TO THE SPIRIT OF NEW ENGLAND

which lives in all that is free, noble, and courageous in America

TIME IN NEW ENGLAND

photographs by   PAUL STRAND

*text selected
and edited by*   NANCY NEWHALL

preface by   PAUL METCALF

afterword by   BEAUMONT NEWHALL

AN APERTURE BOOK

PHOTOGRAPHS COPYRIGHT © 1950, PAUL STRAND; 1977
THE PAUL STRAND FOUNDATION.
TEXT COPYRIGHT © 1950, NANCY NEWHALL; 1977
THE ESTATE OF NANCY NEWHALL.
PREFACE COPYRIGHT © 1980 PAUL METCALF.
AFTERWORD COPYRIGHT © 1980 BEAUMONT NEWHALL.
LIBRARY OF CONGRESS CATALOGUE CARD NO. 80-65763.
ISBN: 0-89381-060-6.
MANUFACTURED IN THE UNITED STATES OF AMERICA.
BOOK DESIGN BY MALCOLM GREAR ASSOCIATES.
JACKET DESIGN BY WENDY BYRNE.

ALL RIGHTS RESERVED UNDER INTERNATIONAL AND PAN-AMERICAN COPYRIGHT CONVENTIONS. PUBLISHED BY APERTURE, INC. DISTRIBUTED IN THE UNITED STATES BY HARPER & ROW, PUBLISHERS, INC., IN THE UNITED KINGDOM, COMMONWEALTH AND OTHER WORLD MARKETS BY PHAIDON PRESS LIMITED, OXFORD; IN CANADA BY VAN NOSTRAND REINHOLD LTD., ONTARIO; AND IN ITALY BY IDEA BOOKS, MILAN.

APERTURE, INC., PUBLISHES A PERIODICAL, PORTFOLIOS, AND BOOKS TO COMMUNICATE WITH SERIOUS PHOTOGRAPHERS AND CREATIVE PEOPLE EVERYWHERE. A COMPLETE CATALOGUE WILL BE MAILED FREE UPON REQUEST. ADDRESS: ELM STREET, MILLERTON, NEW YORK 12546.

TIME IN NEW ENGLAND IS AVAILABLE IN A COLLECTOR'S EDITION OF 450 COPIES, SIGNED AND NUMBERED BY MRS. PAUL STRAND AND BEAUMONT NEWHALL. AN ORIGINAL HAND-PULLED, DUST-GRAIN GRAVURE, IRIS, 1928, ACCOMPANIES THE LIMITED EDITION. EACH GRAVURE IS SIGNED AND APPROVED BY MRS. PAUL STRAND ON BEHALF OF THE PAUL STRAND FOUNDATION.

Contents

Paul Metcalf: *Preface*	13

PART ONE

PHOTOGRAPHS	TEXT	
	1 NEW WORLD	
	John Winthrop: *Aboard the Arbella*	19
Sky and Islands, Prospect Harbor, Maine, 1946		20
Rock by the Sea, Georgetown, Maine, 1925		21
Forest, Maine, 1928		22
	Francis Higginson: *Voyage to New England*	23
	2 WILDERNESS	
	William Bradford: *Arrival—Plymouth, November, 1620*	24
Reef Sea, Prospect Harbor, Maine, 1945		25
Stone Wall in Snow, Stockberger's Farm, 1944		26
Tombstone: *Memento Mori*, Vermont, 1946		27
Burying Ground, Vermont, 1946		28
	John Winthrop: *Winter, 1630*	29
	James Pierpont: *The Spectral Ship*	30
	Edward Johnson: *Planting the Wilderness*	31
	William Bradford: *Sundry Objections against Plymouth Plantation*	32
	Thomas Morton and William Bradford: *Merry Mount*	33
	Anne Bradstreet: *Spirit to Flesh*	35
	3 FOOTHOLD	
Corn, near Brattleboro, Vermont, 1946		36
	Edward Johnson: *New England's Blessings*	37
Apple Orchard, 1946		38
Latch, Vermont, 1944		39
	Edward Johnson: *Boston, 1654*	40
	Massachusetts Law: *Schools*	41
	The New England Primer: *Alphabet*	41
Jack-in-the-Pulpit, 1946		42
	Roger Williams: *Night of Prayer among the Indians*	43
	William Wood: *Birds and Beasts*	44

PHOTOGRAPHS	TEXT	
Decoy, 1946		45
Meeting House Window, 1945		46
	New England's First Fruits	47
	Cotton Mather: *Harvard College in the Seventeenth Century*	48
	William Bradford: *On Learning Hebrew in His Old Age*	49
	Roger Williams: *Foundation of Civil Power*	50

4 QUAKERS

	Edward Johnson: *Warning to Heretics and Libertines*	51
Road, Winter, 1944		52
	George Bishop: *The Whipping of the Quakers*	53
	George Bishop: *Lydia Wardel Goes to Newbury Church as a Sign*	54
	Thomas Wilkie: *The Hanging of the Quaker William Leddra*	54
	Roger Williams: *The Bloody Tenent*	55

5 SAVAGES

Dark Forest, Georgetown, Maine, 1928		56
	Thomas Church: *Pursuit*	57
	Mary Rowlandson: *The Burning of Lancaster*	58
	Cotton Mather: *Hannah Dustan*	59

6 HEAVEN AND HELL

	Cotton Mather: *The Meekness of John Cotton*	61
Church on a Hill, Northern Vermont, 1946		62
	Jonathan Edwards: *Memoir: I am the Rose of Sharon*	63
	Jonathan Edwards: *Sermon: The Eternity of Hell Torments*	64
Tombstone: Winged Skull, Vermont, 1946		65
Leaves, c. 1927		66
	Samuel Sewall: *Diary*	67
	Massachusetts Laws	68
	Essex County Court Records	69

PHOTOGRAPHS	TEXT	
	7 WITCHCRAFT	
Dead Tree, Vermont, 1945		70
	Cotton Mather: *Plague of Evil Angels*	71
	Deodat Lawson: *Witchcraft in Salem Village*	72
Window: Abandoned House, 1944		74
	Margaret Jacobs: *Humble Declaration*	75
	Confession of the Jurors	76

PART TWO

1 NATIVE EARTH

Bunchberry, 1946		78
Church Door, 1946		79
Village on a Salt Marsh, Harrington, Maine, 1946		80
	Samuel Sewall: *Newbury*	81
Farmhouse Window, 1945		82
	Sarah Kemble Knight: *Journey from Boston to New York, 1704*	83
West River Valley, Vermont, 1944		85
Mullen and Stump, Twin Lakes, Connecticut, 1922		86
	Samuel Peters: *Bundling*	87
	Henry Reed Stiles: *Bundling*	88
	Samuel Peters: *The Frogs of Windham: A Tory Satire*	89

2 PROPHECIES

	John Wise: *Democracy*	90
	Samuel Sewall: *The Selling of Joseph*	90
	Nathaniel Ames: *America, 1758*	91

3 REVOLUTION

Town Hall, Vermont, 1946		92
	James Otis: *These Are Their Bounds*	93
	John Adams: *The Year 1765*	94
	A Son of Liberty: *Dedication of a Tree of Liberty*	94
	The Boston Massacre	95
	John Adams: *Chrispus Attucks to Thomas Hutchinson*	96

PHOTOGRAPHS	TEXT	
Splitting Granite, 1945		97
	John Adams: *After Town Meeting*	98
	Samuel Adams: *The Liberties of America*	98
	Samuel Adams: *Tea Party*	99
	Samuel Adams: *Closing of Boston Port*	99
Bell Rope, Massachusetts, 1945		100
Village, Vermont, 1946		101
	Paul Revere: *His Own Story*	102
	Ephraim Banks: *Diary of a Revolutionary Soldier*	104
Graveyard and Mountain, East Jamaica, Vermont, 1944		105
Corn Crib, West River Valley, Vermont, 1944		106
	Ethan Allen: *Ticonderoga*	107
	Henry W. DePuy: *Trial of a Tory in Vermont*	108
	Abigail Adams: *To Her Husband, John Adams*	108
	John Adams: *Drafting the Declaration of Independence*	109
Eagle, 1946		110

PART THREE

1 HILL AND TOWN

	Samuel Davis: *Journey to Connecticut, 1789*	112
	Nathan Perkins: *Journey to Vermont, 1789*	113
Open Door, 1945		114
	Eliza Southgate Bowne: *Winter Dance*	115
	Lucy Larcom: *Mill-Girl*	117
Textile Mill, 1946		118
The River, Maine, 1946		119
	Seba Smith: *Huckler's Row*	120
	Elihu Burritt: *Diary of the Learned Blacksmith*	121
	Ralph Waldo Emerson: *Ezra Ripley, D.D.*	122
By the Sea, Maine, 1945		123
Spruce and Lichen, Maine, 1945		124
	Ralph Waldo Emerson: *Mary Moody Emerson*	125

2 THE SEA

	Seargent Smith Prentiss: *The Sons of New England*	127
Whale Ship, Mystic, Connecticut, 1946		128

PHOTOGRAPHS	TEXT	
	Advice to a Boy Going to Sea	129
	Sea Chantey: *A Yankee Ship*	129
	Cargoes Unloading in Salem Harbor	129
Sea and Sky, near Prospect Harbor, Maine, 1946		130
Figurehead: *Samuel Piper*, 1946		131
	Lord Timothy Dexter: *How He Came to Fortune*	132
	New England Clipper Ships and Voyages	133
	Richard Henry Dana, Jr.: *Furling Sail off Cape Horn*	134
	Herman Melville: *Letter to Evert Duyckinck*	134
	Herman Melville: *Whale Hunt*	135
	Obed Macy: *The Whale Ship* Essex	136
Open Sea, Maine, 1946		137
Wreck: Timber and Snails, 1928		138
Seaweed, Maine, 1928		139
	Owen Chase: *Survivors in the Mate's Boat*	140
Tombstone: Death the Victor, Vermont, 1946		141
	William Bentley: *Prayers for Salem*	142
Figurehead attributed to Samuel MacIntyre: *Lady with a Medallion*, 1946		143
	Richard Henry Dana, Jr.: *Full Sail*	144

3 FINE AURORAS

	Ralph Waldo Emerson: *Poetry Has Been Written This Very Day*	145
	Ralph Waldo Emerson: *Adam in The Garden*	146
	Henry David Thoreau: *Morning*	146
Mullen, Maine, 1927		147
	Henry David Thoreau: *Walden Pond*	148
Cobweb in Rain, Georgetown, Maine, 1927		149
	Emily Dickinson: *Hummingbird*	150
	Emily Dickinson: *Cocoon*	150
Fern, Early Morning, Georgetown, Maine, 1927		151
	Nathaniel Hawthorne: *To Sophia*	152
	Nathaniel Hawthorne: *Note-Book*	153
Dried Seaweed, 1946		154
By the Sea, Maine, 1945		155
	Margaret Fuller: *A Man's Ambition*	156

PHOTOGRAPHS	TEXT	
	Nathaniel Hawthorne: *Martha Hunt*	157
	Emily Dickinson: *Poems*	159
	Herman Melville: *Letter to Hawthorne*	160
Sea-worn Driftwood, 1929		162
	Herman Melville: *All Visible Objects*	163

4 PROTEST

Mr. Bennett, Vermont, 1944		164
	Henry David Thoreau: *A Born Protestant*	165
	Henry David Thoreau: *Freedom to Be Free*	166
	Susan B. Anthony: *Rights of Woman*	167
	William Cullen Bryant: *The Right to Strike, 1836*	167
Beatrice Albee, Prospect Harbor, Maine, 1946		168
Mill Dam, Vermont, 1945		169
	Harriet H. Robinson: *Turn-Out, 1836*	170
	Wendell Phillips: *New England and the Labor Movement*	171
Stone Mill, 1946		172
Harry Wass, Cape Split, Maine, 1946		173
	Orestes Brownson: *Democracy and Society, 1840*	174
	Theodore Parker: *The March of Human Freedom*	175

5 ABOLITION

Driftwood: Dark Roots, Maine, 1929		176
	William Fairfield: *To His Mother*	177
	Samuel Gridley Howe: *To Charles Sumner*	178
	Daniel Webster: *To John Taylor*	179
Steeple, 1946		180
	William Lloyd Garrison: *To the Public*	181
	Meeting of the Boston Female Anti-Slavery Society	182
Meeting House Door, 1945		184
Louis Cole, Prospect Harbor, Maine, 1946		185
	Wendell Phillips: *The Murder of Lovejoy*	186
	Theodore Parker: *May, 1851*	187
	Thomas Wentworth Higginson: *The Rescue of Shadrach*	187
	Thomas Wentworth Higginson: *Plot to Rescue Anthony Burns*	188

PHOTOGRAPHS	TEXT	
	Thomas Wentworth Higginson: *John Brown's Household*, 1859	190
Rock, Cape Split, Maine, 1946		192
Apple Tree, Full Bloom, 1946		193
	Henry David Thoreau: *A Plea for Captain John Brown*	194

PART FOUR

1 EBB

Toadstool and Grasses, Maine, 1928		196
	Ralph Waldo Emerson: *It Is the Age of Severance*	197
	Henry Adams: *Return*, 1868	198
	Charles Francis Adams: *Boston and Quincy*	199
Palladian Window, Maine, 1945		200
Bertha Moore, Prospect Harbor, Maine, 1946		201
Closed Door, Maine, 1945		202
	Thomas Wentworth Higginson: *The Funeral of Emily Dickinson*	203
Parlor, Prospect Harbor, Maine, 1946		204
Little Dead Tree, 1946		205
	Edwin Arlington Robinson: *Richard Cory*	206
Empty House, 1945		207
Old Farm, Maine, 1945		208
	Ed Pendexter: *Letters*	209
Corea, Maine, 1945		210
	Robert Frost: *An Old Man's Winter Night*	211

2 TENACIOUS ROOTS

Spruce and Rock, Maine, 1946		212
	Winslow Homer: *Letters from Prout's Neck, Maine*	213
	Sarah Orne Jewett: *Maine Fishermen*	214
Fish Houses, Corea, Maine, 1945		215
Leo Wass, Cape Split, Maine, 1946		216
Interior: Stove, Prospect Harbor, Maine, 1946		217
	Sarah Orne Jewett: *By the Morning Boat*	218
Susan Thompson, Cape Split, Maine, 1945		219
The Dock, 1945		220

PHOTOGRAPHS	TEXT	
	Cape Cod Folk Tale: *Jedidy and the Devil*	221
Trawlers, Maine, 1946		224
Merrill Spurling, Prospect Harbor, Maine, 1946		225
	William James: *Walk in Boston*	226
	Henry Adams: *Winter and Summer*	227
Children, Vermont, 1944		228
Side Porch, Vermont, 1946		229
The Little Sail, Prospect Harbor, Maine, 1946		230
	Marsden Hartley: *A Painting by Ryder*	231
	Miriam Colwell: *Poem*	231
Beachgrass, Maine, 1946		232
Belle Crowley, 1946		233
Woods, Maine, 1945		234
	Genevieve Taggard: *The Nursery Rhyme and the Summer Visitor*	235
	Amy Lowell: *Lilacs*	236
Hope Noonan, 1946		238
House and Appleblossoms, 1946		239
	Thomas Wolfe: *Journey to the North*	240
	3 AFFIRMATIONS	
	Genevieve Taggard: *To Ethan Allen*	241
Midwinter, 1946		242
Towards the Sugar House, Vermont, 1944		243
Tombstone and Sky, 1946		244
	Justice Oliver Wendell Holmes: *Dead, Yet Living*	245
	Nicola Sacco: *To His Son, Dante*	246
	Bartolomeo Vanzetti: *After Receiving Sentence of Death*	246
Iris, Georgetown, Maine, 1928		247
	W. E. Burghardt Du Bois: *I Dream of a World*	248
	Norman Corwin: *The Horsemen of Apocalypse*	248
	Conrad Aiken: *Mayflower*	249
	Van Wyck Brooks: *New England*	250
Wild Iris, Maine, 1927		251
Church, Vermont, 1944		252
	Beaumont Newhall: *Afterword*	253
	Additional Source Notes	255

Preface

That the study of man is the study of migration, is not a particularly novel idea. From primitive man, wandering in search of food and in the process peopling the world, through the historic era—the waves of raid and conquest, crusade and retreat—man clearly has lived in an unsettled state.

In the book *The Golden Door,*[1] the authors point out that migrations in the modern era have presented a somewhat different picture:

> "In certain respects the modern pattern of movement is a distinctly different kind of migration from the kinds that predominated in the centuries after the fall of Rome. The most important difference is that the decision to move was usually taken independently by an individual or by the head of a family for that family. Occasionally, small groups, such as the Puritan settlers of New England, moved as a group, but they were more the exception than the rule."

From the viewpoint of American history, this distinction between the Puritans and other settlers is of significance. As a group or communal movement, the Puritans alone among the major settlers submerged individual ambition in the welfare of the community. Although the exigencies in all the early settlements up and down the Atlantic coast forced individuals into a kind of loose, neighborly cooperation—the spirit of openness and friendliness that survives in the Midwest and West today—the Puritans alone established themselves as a potent unitary force.

They came to these shores to establish the Kingdom of Heaven on Earth. This was no metaphor: it was a literal, overriding, single energy, governing every daily thought and act. As a corollary, and quite beside the point in their own consciousness, they found themselves taking America seriously in a way unique among all the settlers. For them, the dreadful ocean that they had crossed, separating them from England and the Church of England, was a barrier at their backs. The Southerner, by contrast, had never in his heart and mind left England. He had brought a piece of it with him, planted it in America, with ties to King and Archbishop unbroken. Neither were the Puritans motivated by greed. They had no desire to raid, get rich, and go home (a desire, incidentally, that bedeviled Christopher Columbus among the "gentlemen" who wished to join him on his voyages, and that governed much early Spanish settlement).

It has even been claimed that the American Revolution was in fact effected by the Puritans, the Separatists. They broke the spiritual ties with the mother country, creating a separation of which the events of 1776 and afterward were a political and economic confirmation.

The Puritans' plan embodied a theocratic dynamic, verging on the demonic, that ensured the success of their settlement and generated influences and repercussions with an impact felt well past their own day.

> "Consider that there are no persons in all the world unto whom God speaketh by His Providence as he doth to us."

> "Have you not observed that there have been more awfull tremendous dispensations of divine Providence in New-England than in any place else?"

> "There never was a Generation that did so perfectly shake off the dust of Babylon . . . nor a place so like unto New Jerusalem as New England."

> "How wonderfully suited is the going of Christ into America."

> "If we look abroad over the face of the whole earth,

[1] *The Golden Door,* Paul R. Ehrlich, Loy Bilderback, and Anne H. Ehrlich, (New York: Ballantine Books, 1979).

where shall we see a place or people brought to such perfection?"

"The *New English* Churches are a preface to the New Heavens."[2]

Such were the stated beliefs of the Puritans.

Then, a significant change occurred. After the initial years of struggle, working a "remote, rocky, bushy, barren, wild-woody soil," the settlements began to be successful—Indians driven back, crops secure, the beginnings of a fishing industry, and the first stages of expansion. The intense spiritual rigors began to yield, to make accommodation for this new phenomenon of temporal success. There was a period of delicate, almost seamless transition, in which the Puritans' self-assurance, not to say arrogance, served them well:

"Look upon our townes & fields, look upon our habitations & shops and ships and behold our numerous posterity, and great encrease in the blessings of the Land & Sea. . . . Yes, there is not only a *spiritual glory*, visible onto to a spiritual eye, but also an *externall, and visible glory*."

"The gospel hath brought in its right hand Eternal Salvation. And in its left hand, Riches with Protection and Deliverance from Enemies."

"The Blessings both of the *upper and nether Springs*, the Blessings of Time and of Eternity."

"Such parents as have entered into a Covenant with the Lord may be assured, that the virtue, the blessing, the efficacy of the Covenant shall never be disannuled, but it shall go on to your children forever; by your Covenant, you have such a hold of God, that you may be assured, he will be a God, not to you only, but your seed shall stand before the Lord, to serve him for ever."[3]

Thus, the *Arbella* and the *Mayflower* yielded to the Oriental trade and the whaling industry, and the "barren, wild-woody soil" yielded to Beacon Hill, Boston Brahmins, and Boston banks, with the sons of sons of sons blessed in perpetuity.

New England became an export item. Look at the place names across the country: in Ohio alone there are Plymouth and New Plymouth, Lexington and New Lexington, Springfield and New Springfield, Weston and New Weston; the principal city of Oregon is Portland, its capital Salem.

Still, for all the transition, the graceful acceptance of temporal glory, the old rigorous spirit—dour, perhaps injured—survived in New England as nowhere else. One is reminded of the encapsulated life of Emily Dickinson. Those other Nineteenth-Century figures—Thoreau, Hawthorne, Emerson—could be penetrating, perhaps soaring, certainly acute; but they would not invite description as full-bodied, or full-blooded. Melville was an exception here, but it is well to remember that Melville was only half Yankee; on his mother's side he was Dutch and had in fact, been raised in New York City and Albany.

Hawthorne was a major father figure for Melville, but the rush and enthusiasm of Melville's spirit overwhelmed the reserved Hawthorne. Later, Melville wrote that there was something lacking in the "plump sphericity" of Hawthorne.

Certainly there was never a more characteristic latter-day Puritan than John Brown: an awesome mix, well-nigh unbelievable in one man, of casual cruelty, intense and narrow passion, and the loftiest of ideals. The entire Abolitionist movement, in fact, was a New England project—a well-formed recrudescence of the Puritan ethic.

[2]The excerpts from Puritan texts may be found in two books by Sacvan Bercovitch: *The Puritan Origins of the American Self* (New Haven: Yale University Press, 1975), and *The American Jeremiad* (Madison: University of Wisconsin Press, 1978). [3]Ibid.

One of the clearest testaments to the power of the Puritan spirit is the evidence of what happened to some of its bearers as they departed westward out of New England: the flurry of strange sects, blossoming as the borders of New York, Ohio, and Indiana were crossed. Shakers, Mormons, Campbellites, Millerites. Ideal communities at Oneida, New York, and New Harmony, Indiana, the former offering free love, and perhaps incest. Having escaped the Calvinist umbrella, these people were like children suddenly let out of school.

* * *

One of the lovelier quotations in this book is from the diary of a revolutionary soldier—a farmer from Concord: "I like not these New York people, for they are craven and servile and filled with a lust for their property. Too much owning is a curse in a man's blood." New Englanders had a genuine hostility for people other than themselves; one is tempted to call it xenophobia. And this hostility seemed to focus particularly on New Yorkers. Hawthorne says somewhere that Melville could never seem to be at peace with himself; perhaps this was because Melville contained both hostile factions in his own blood.

Outsiders are often attracted to New England: they enter, submerge, and identify. But there is another kind of outsider who is attracted to New England, who comes to understand it as New Englanders themselves, or those who have entered, submerged, and identified, cannot. Such is Paul Strand, son of Jacob, native New Yorker through and through.

The lyric sense of nature, the stark theocratic purity, the practical sensibility, the unmatched craftsmanship, the careful affluence—all traceable to the establishment of the Kingdom of Heaven on Earth and its orderly transitions—all of these are clear in the photographs that Strand, the matchless craftsman, brought back from his excursions to New England.

* * *

In 1759, Nathaniel Ames, resident in Boston, wrote as follows:

"O ye unborn inhabitants of America! Should this page escape its destined conflagration at the year's end, and these alphabetical letters remain legible—when your eyes behold the sun after he has rolled the seasons round for two or three centuries more, you will know that in Anno Domini 1758, we dreamed of your times."

Perhaps it was of Nancy Newhall and Paul Strand that Nathaniel Ames dreamed. Nancy Newhall, trained and setting out as a painter, instead early in her career threw all her energies into writing about photography, endeavoring to bring to this medium, to the best of those who worked in it, the dignity and recognition long accorded to painters. Besides Strand, she researched, and worked with such as Stieglitz, the Westons, and Ansel Adams. For this book, however, she was seeking a new form: mining the documents, thrusting them side by side with the images brought back by Paul Strand—the New Yorker with his magic box and chemicals—"to create a portrait more dynamic than either medium could present alone."

Newhall and Strand agreed on a common ground, then pursued individual modes or trails, the two never melding, never yielding to one another. Rather, the text creates images in the mind, begging to be seen, and the photographs push into the head, driving toward expression. Newhall and Strand have reified this New England in which Nathaniel Ames and his forebears had established a divine plan, a temporal force, a world apart from England, and a place in its own right—an ideosyncratic continuum.

PAUL METCALF

PART ONE

I *New World*

Aboard the Arbella

Approaching New England, 1630

For this end we must be knit together as one man. We must entertain each other in brotherly affection. We must be willing to abridge ourselves of our superfluities for the supply of others' necessities. We must delight in each other; make others' conditions our own; rejoice together, mourn together, labor and suffer together, as members of the same body. So shall we keep the unity of the spirit in the bond of peace.

The Lord will be our God, and delight to dwell among us as His own people; when He shall make us a praise and glory, that men shall say of succeeding plantations, 'The Lord make it likely that of New England.'

For we must consider that we shall be as a city upon a hill. The eyes of all people are upon us.

JOHN WINTHROP
A Model of Christian Charity, 1630.

Voyage to New England

June 24, 1629. Wednesday.

Wind north-east, a fair day and clear. This day we all had a clear and comfortable sight of America, and of the Cape Sable, seven or eight leagues northward. Here we saw yellow gilliflowers on the sea.

Thursday.

In the afternoon we had a clear sight of many islands and hills by the seashore. Now we saw a great store of great whales, puffing up water as they go; some of them came near our ship. Their backs appeared like a little island.

Friday.

A foggy morning, but after clear, and wind calm. We saw many schools of mackerel, infinite multitudes on every side of our ship. The sea was abundantly stored with rockweed and yellow flowers, like gilliflowers.

By noon we were within three leagues of Cape Ann; and as we sailed along the coast, we saw every hill and dale and every island full of gay woods and high trees. The nearer we came to the shore, the more flowers in abundance, sometimes scattered abroad, sometimes joined in sheets nine or ten yards long, which we supposed to be brought from the low meadows by the tide.

Now what with fine woods and green trees by land and these yellow flowers painting the sea, made us all desirous to see our new paradise of New-England, when we saw such forerunning signals of fertility afar off.

Saturday.

About four o'clock, having with much pain compassed the harbor, there came a fearful gust of wind and rain and thunder and lightning, with no little terror and trouble to our mariners to loose down the sails when the fury of the storm struck us. But, blessed be God, He soon removed this storm, and it was a fair and sweet evening.

A westerly wind brought us, between five and six o'clock, to a fine harbor, seven miles from the head point of Cape Ann, where there was an island, whither four of our men with a boat went, and brought back again ripe strawberries and gooseberries, and single sweet roses.

FRANCIS HIGGINSON
'A True Relation of the Last Voyage to New-England,' 1629.

2 *Wilderness*

Arrival at Plymouth, November, 1620

Being thus arrived in a good harbor and brought safe to land, they fell upon their knees and blessed the God of Heaven, who had brought them over the vast and furious ocean, and delivered them from all the perils and miseries thereof, again to set their feet on the firm and stable earth, their proper element.

They had now no friends to welcome them, nor inns to entertain or refresh their weatherbeaten bodies, no houses or much less towns to repair to, to seek for succor. And for the season, it was winter, and they that know the winters of that country know them to be sharp and violent, and subject to cruel and fierce storms, dangerous to travel to known places, much more to search an unknown coast. Besides, what could they see but a hideous and desolate wilderness, full of wild beasts and wild men? Neither could they, as it were, go up to the top of Pisgah, to view from their wilderness a more goodly country to feed their hopes; for which way soever they turned their eyes (save upwards to the heavens) they could have little solace or content in respect of any outward objects. For summer being done, all things stand upon them with a weatherbeaten face; and the whole country, full of woods and thickets, represented a wild and savage hue. If they looked behind them, there was the mighty ocean which they had passed, and was now as a main bar and gulf to separate them from all the civil parts of the world.

GOVERNOR WILLIAM BRADFORD
Of Plymouth Plantation.

Winter, 1630

December 24.

This day the wind came N.W., very strong, and some snow withal, but so cold as some had their fingers frozen.

December 26.

The rivers were frozen up, and they of Charlestown could not come to the sermon at Boston till the afternoon at high tide.

December 28.

Richard Garrett, a shoemaker of Salem, with one of his daughters, a young maid, and four others, went towards Plymouth in a shallop. And about the Gurnett's Nose the wind overblew so much at N.W. as they were forced to come to a killock* at twenty fathoms, but their boat drave and shaked out the stone, and they were put to sea. And the boat took in much water, which did freeze so hard as they could not free her. But one of their company espying land near Cape Cod, they made shift to hoist part of their sail, and, by God's special providence, were carried through the rocks to the shore, where some gat on land, but some had their legs frozen into the ice, so as they were forced to be cut out. Being come on shore, they were forced to lie in the open air all night. In the morning, two of their company went toward Plymouth, supposing it had been within seven or eight miles, whereas it was near fifty miles from them.

By the way they met two Indian squaws, who, coming home, told their husbands that they had met two Englishmen. They made after them, and brought them back to their wigwams, and entertained them kindly. And one of them went with them the next day to Plymouth, and the other went to find out their boat and the rest of their company, which were seven miles off. And having found them, he holp them what he could, and returned to his wigwam, and fetched a hatchet, and built them a wigwam and covered it, and gat them wood, for they were so weak and frozen as they could not stir.

And Garrett died about two days after his landing. And the ground being so frozen as they could not dig his grave, the Indian hewed a hole about half a yard deep with his hatchet, and having laid the corpse in it, he laid over it a great heap of wood to keep it from the wolves.

February 9.

The *Lyon* came to an anchor before Boston, where she rode very well, not withstanding the great drift of ice.

February 10.

The frost brake up; and after that, though we had many snows and sharp frosts, yet they continued not; neither were the waters frozen up as before. The poorer sort of people, who lay long in tents, etc., were much afflicted with the scurvy, and many died, especially at Boston and Charlestown. But when this ship came and brought store of juice of lemons, many recovered speedily. It hath always been observed here that such as fell into discontent and lingered after their former condition in England, fell into the scurvy and died.

*Rude anchor: a stone in a wooden frame.

JOHN WINTHROP
The History of New England from 1630-1649.

The Spectral Ship

A letter to Cotton Mather from the pastor at New Haven.

Reverend and dear Sir:

In compliance with your desires, I now give you the relation of that APPARITION OF A SHIP IN THE AIR, which I have received from the most credible, judicious, and curious surviving observers of it.

In the year 1647, besides much other lading, a far more rich treasure of passengers put themselves on board a new ship, built at Rhode Island, of about 150 tons; but so walty that the master often said she would prove their grave. In the month of January, cutting their way through much ice, with many fears as well as prayers and tears, they set sail.

The spring following, no tidings of these friends arrived with the ships from England. New Haven's heart began to fail her. This put the godly people on much prayer, both public and private, 'That the Lord would let them hear what He had done with their dear friends.'

In June next ensuing, a great thunder-storm arose out of the northwest, after which, the hemisphere being serene, about an hour before sunset, a SHIP of like dimensions with the aforesaid, with her canvas and colors abroad, appeared in the air coming up from our harbor's mouth, which lies southward from the town, seemingly with her sails filled under a fresh gale, sailing against the wind for the space of half an hour.

Many were drawn to behold the great work of God; yea, the very children cried out, 'There's a brave ship!' At length, crowding up so near some of the spectators, as that they imagined a man might hurl a stone on board her, her maintop seemed to be blown off, but left hanging in the shrouds; then her mizzentop; then all her mastings seemed blown away by the board. Quickly after her hulk brought unto a careen, she overset, and so vanished into a smoky cloud, which in some time dissipated, leaving, as everywhere else, a clear air.

The admiring spectators could distinguish the several colors of each part, the principal rigging, and such proportions as caused not only the generality of persons to say, 'This was the mould of their ship, and thus was her tragic end,' but Mr Davenport also in public declared 'That God had condescended for the quieting of their afflicted spirits, this extraordinary account of his sovereign disposal of those for whom so many fervent prayers were made continually.'

Thus I am, Sir, your humble servant.
James Pierpont

JAMES PIERPONT
Quoted by Cotton Mather in *Magnalia Christi Americana*, London, 1702.

Planting the Wilderness: The Town of Concord

The land they purchase of the Indians, and, with much difficulties, they discover the fitness of the place, sometimes passing through the thickets, where their hands are forced to make way for their bodies' passage, and their feet clambering over the crossed trees, which, when they missed, they sunk to an uncertain bottom in water. The ragged bushes scratch their legs foully; some have had the blood trickle down at every step. And in the time of summer, the sun casts such a reflecting heat from the sweet fern, whose scent is very strong, so that some herewith have been very near fainting. And this not be endured for one day, but for many. And verily, did not the Lord encourage their natural parts with hopes of a new and strong and strange discovery—expecting every hour to see some rare sight never seen before—they were never able to hold out and break through.

Their further hardship is to travel sometimes they know not whither. Bewildered indeed without sight of sun, their compass miscarrying in crowding through the bushes, they sadly search up and down for a known way,—the Indians' paths being not above one foot broad, so that a man may travel many days and never find one.

After they have thus found out a place of abode, they burrow themselves into the earth for their first shelter, under some hillside. Casting the earth aloft upon timber, they make a smoky fire against the earth at the highest side. And thus these poor servants of Christ provide shelter for themselves, their wives, and little ones, keeping off the short showers from their lodgings. But the long rains penetrate through, to their great disturbance in the night season. Yet in these poor wigwams they sing psalms, pray, and praise their God, till they can provide them houses. Which ordinarily was not wont to be with many until the earth, by the Lord's blessing, brought forth bread to feed them, their wives, and little ones. Which with sore labors they attain, everyone that can lift a hoe to strike it into the earth standing stoutly to their labors, and tear up the roots and bushes.

CAPTAIN EDWARD JOHNSON
Wonder-Working Providence of Sion's Saviour, London, 1654.

lived stragglingly, and were of no strength in any place. But insolently he persisted, and threatened withal that if any came to molest him, let them look to themselves. So they obtained of the Governor of Plymouth to send Captain Standish, and some other aid with him, to take Morton by force. They found him to stand stiffly in his defence, having made fast his doors, armed his consorts, set divers dishes of powder and bullets ready on the table. They summoned him to yield, but he kept his house, and they could get nothing but scoffs and scorns from him. At length, fearing some violence to the house, he and some of his crew came out, not to yield but to shoot, so steeled with drink as their pieces were too heavy for them. Himself with a carbine had thought to have shot Captain Standish; but he stepped to him, and put by his piece, and took him. Neither was there any hurt done to any of either side, save that one was so drunk that he ran his own nose upon the point of a sword that one held before him as he entered the house.

Morton: The Separatists [Pilgrims] envying the prosperity and hope of the plantation at Ma-re Mount (which they perceived to be in a good way for gain in the beaver trade) conspired together against mine host. And taking advantage of the time when his company were gone up into the islands, to trade with the savages for beaver, they set upon mine host at a place called Wessaguscus, where by accident they found him all alone. The conspirators were so jocund that they feasted their bodies, and fell to tippling. Mine host feigned grief, and could not be persuaded either to eat or drink. In the dead of night, up gets mine host and got to the second door that he was to pass; and shut it after him with such violence that it affrighted some of the conspirators. The word was, 'Oh, he's gone, he's gone! What shall we do?' The rest, half asleep, start up in a maze, and like rams, ran their heads at one another full butt in the dark. Their grand leader, Captain Shrimp, took on most furiously, and tore his clothes for anger, to see the empty nest and their bird gone.

In the meantime mine host was got home to Ma-re Mount through the woods, eight miles, finding his way by the help of the lightning. And there he prepared powder three pounds dried, and four good guns for him and the two assistants left at his house, with bullets of several sizes. One of mine host's men proved a craven; the other had proved his wits to purchase a little valor, before mine host had observed his posture.

The nine worthies coming before the den of this supposed monster began, like Don Quixote against the windmill, to beat a parley, and to offer quarter if mine host should yield. But he, having taken up his arms in his just defence, replied that he would not lay by those arms. Yet to save the effusion of so much worthy blood as would have issued out of the veins of these nine worthies of New Canaan, if mine host should have played upon them out of his portholes (for they came within danger like a flock of wild geese, as if they had been tailored one to another), mine host was content to yield upon a quarter. But mine host no sooner had set open the door and issued out but instantly Captain Shrimp and the rest and the worthies laid hold of his arms and had him down, and so eagerly was every man bent against him that they would have a slice with scabbard and all for haste, until an old soldier that was there by accident, clapped his gun under the weapons, and sharply rebuked these worthies for their unworthy practices.

WILLIAM BRADFORD
Of Plymouth Plantation.

THOMAS MORTON
New English Canaan, Amsterdam, 1637.

Planting the Wilderness: The Town of Concord

The land they purchase of the Indians, and, with much difficulties, they discover the fitness of the place, sometimes passing through the thickets, where their hands are forced to make way for their bodies' passage, and their feet clambering over the crossed trees, which, when they missed, they sunk to an uncertain bottom in water. The ragged bushes scratch their legs foully; some have had the blood trickle down at every step. And in the time of summer, the sun casts such a reflecting heat from the sweet fern, whose scent is very strong, so that some herewith have been very near fainting. And this not be endured for one day, but for many. And verily, did not the Lord encourage their natural parts with hopes of a new and strong and strange discovery—expecting every hour to see some rare sight never seen before—they were never able to hold out and break through.

Their further hardship is to travel sometimes they know not whither. Bewildered indeed without sight of sun, their compass miscarrying in crowding through the bushes, they sadly search up and down for a known way,—the Indians' paths being not above one foot broad, so that a man may travel many days and never find one.

After they have thus found out a place of abode, they burrow themselves into the earth for their first shelter, under some hillside. Casting the earth aloft upon timber, they make a smoky fire against the earth at the highest side. And thus these poor servants of Christ provide shelter for themselves, their wives, and little ones, keeping off the short showers from their lodgings. But the long rains penetrate through, to their great disturbance in the night season. Yet in these poor wigwams they sing psalms, pray, and praise their God, till they can provide them houses. Which ordinarily was not wont to be with many until the earth, by the Lord's blessing, brought forth bread to feed them, their wives, and little ones. Which with sore labors they attain, everyone that can lift a hoe to strike it into the earth standing stoutly to their labors, and tear up the roots and bushes.

CAPTAIN EDWARD JOHNSON
Wonder-Working Providence of Sion's Saviour, London, 1654.

Sundry Objections Against Plymouth Plantation

Objection: The water is not wholesome.

Answer: If they mean not so wholesome as the good beer and wine in London (which they dearly love) we will not dispute with them; but else, for water, it is as good as any in the world, and it is wholesome enough to us that can be content therewith.

Objection: Many of the particular members of the plantation will not work for the general.

Answer: This also is not wholly true; for though some do it not willingly, and others not honestly, yet all do it; and he that doth worst gets his own food and something besides. But we will not excuse them, but labor to reform them, or else to quit the plantation of them.

Objection: Many of them are thievish and steal one from another.

Answer: Would London had been free from that crime! Then we should not have been troubled with these here; it is well known sundry have smarted well for it, and so are the rest like to do, if they be taken.

Objection: The people are much annoyed with mosquitoes.

Answer: They are too delicate and unfit to begin new plantations and colonies that cannot endure the biting of a mosquito; we would wish such to keep at home till at least they be mosquito proof.

GOVERNOR WILLIAM BRADFORD
Of Plymouth Plantation.

Merry Mount

NOTE: The wrath of the Plymouth colony was aroused by certain practices, social, moral, and commercial, of a nearby plantation, whose proprietors were by no means Pilgrims or Puritans. Thomas Morton, during the absence of his partners in Virginia, where they were selling the time of their bondservants, seized control of the plantation, freed the remaining servants, and received them as his equals. The accounts left by Bradford, Governor of Plymouth, and by Morton, Lord of Merry Mount, are here presented for their differences.

I. *The Maypole*

Governor William Bradford: And Morton became lord of misrule. And after they had got some goods into their hands, much by trading with the Indians, they spent it in quaffing and drinking both wine and strong waters, ten shillings worth in a morning. They also set up a Maypole, drinking and dancing about it many days together, inviting the Indian women for their consorts, dancing and drinking together like so many fairies or furies rather, and worse practices, as if they had anew revived and celebrated the feast of the Roman goddess Flora, or the beastly practices of the mad Bacchanalians. And Morton composed sundry rhymes and verses, tending to lasciviousness and to the detraction and scandal of some persons, which he affixed to this idle or idol Maypole. They changed also the name of their place; they call it Merry Mount, as if this jollity would have lasted forever.

Thomas Morton: The inhabitants prepared to set up a Maypole and therefore brewed a barrel of excellent beer, and provided a case of bottles to be spent, with other good cheer, for all comers. And upon May Day they brought the Maypole to the place appointed, with drums, guns, pistols, and other fitting instruments; and there erected it with the help of savages, that came thither of purpose to see the manner of our revels. A goodly pine-tree of eighty feet long was reared up, with a pair of buck's horns nailed on near unto the top of it, a fair sea-mark how to find out the way to mine host of Ma-re Mount. There was likewise a merry song made, sung with a chorus, every man bearing his part, hand in hand about the Maypole:

> Make green garlands, bring bottles out;
> And fill sweet nectar freely about;
> Uncover thy head and fear no harm,
> For here's good liquor to keep it warm.
>
> Give to the nymph that's free from scorn
> No Irish stuff nor Scotch overworn.
> Lasses in beaver coats, come away;
> Ye shall be welcome to us night and day.
>   *Chorus*
> Drink and be merry, merry, merry, boys.
> Let all your delight be in Hymen's joys.

II. *The Capture*

Bradford: Now, to maintain this riotous prodigality and profuse excess, Morton, hearing what gain the French and fishermen made by the trading of pieces, powder and shot to the Indians, he began the same; and first he taught them how to charge and discharge, and what shot to use for fowl and what for deer. His neighbors meeting the Indians in the woods armed with guns, it was a terror to them who lived stragglingly, and were of no strength in any place. But insolently he persisted, and threatened withal that if any came to molest him, let them look to themselves. So they obtained of the Governor of Plymouth to send Captain Standish, and some other aid with him, to take Morton by force. They found him to stand stiffly in his defence, having made fast his doors, armed his consorts, set divers dishes of powder and bullets ready on the table. They summoned him to yield, but he kept his house, and they could get nothing but scoffs and scorns from him. At length, fearing some violence to the house, he and some of his crew came out, not to yield but to shoot, so steeled with drink as their pieces were too heavy for them. Himself with a carbine had thought to have shot Captain Standish; but he stepped to him, and put by his piece, and took him. Neither was there any hurt done to any of either side, save that one was so drunk that he ran his own nose upon the point of a sword that one held before him as he entered the house.

Morton: The Separatists [Pilgrims] envying the prosperity and hope of the plantation at Ma-re Mount (which they perceived to be in a good way for gain in the beaver trade) conspired together against mine host. And taking advantage of the time when his company were gone up into the islands, to trade with the savages for beaver, they set upon mine host at a place called Wessaguscus, where by accident they found him all alone. The conspirators were so jocund that they feasted their bodies, and fell to tippling. Mine host feigned grief, and could not be persuaded either to eat or drink. In the dead of night, up gets mine host and got to the second door that he was to pass; and shut it after him with such violence that it affrighted some of the conspirators. The word was, 'Oh, he's gone, he's gone! What shall we do?' The rest, half asleep, start up in a maze, and like rams, ran their heads at one another full butt in the dark. Their grand leader, Captain Shrimp, took on most furiously, and tore his clothes for anger, to see the empty nest and their bird gone.

In the meantime mine host was got home to Ma-re Mount through the woods, eight miles, finding his way by the help of the lightning. And there he prepared powder three pounds dried, and four good guns for him and the two assistants left at his house, with bullets of several sizes. One of mine host's men proved a craven; the other had proved his wits to purchase a little valor, before mine host had observed his posture.

The nine worthies coming before the den of this supposed monster began, like Don Quixote against the windmill, to beat a parley, and to offer quarter if mine host should yield. But he, having taken up his arms in his just defence, replied that he would not lay by those arms. Yet to save the effusion of so much worthy blood as would have issued out of the veins of these nine worthies of New Canaan, if mine host should have played upon them out of his portholes (for they came within danger like a flock of wild geese, as if they had been tailored one to another), mine host was content to yield upon a quarter. But mine host no sooner had set open the door and issued out but instantly Captain Shrimp and the rest and the worthies laid hold of his arms and had him down, and so eagerly was every man bent against him that they would have a slice with scabbard and all for haste, until an old soldier that was there by accident, clapped his gun under the weapons, and sharply rebuked these worthies for their unworthy practices.

WILLIAM BRADFORD
Of Plymouth Plantation.

THOMAS MORTON
New English Canaan, Amsterdam, 1637.

Spirit to Flesh

Be still, thou unregenerate part;
Disturb no more my settled heart,
For I have vowed, and so will do,
Thee as a foe still to pursue.
Sisters we are, yea, twins we be,
Yet deadly feud 'twixt thee and me.
Thou speakest me fair, but hatest me sore;
Thy flattering shows I'll trust no more.
How oft thy slave hast thou me made
When I believed what thou hast said.
I'll stop mine ears at these thy charms,
And count them for my deadly harms.
My greatest honor it shall be
When I am victor over thee.

ANNE BRADSTREET
'The Flesh and the Spirit,' *Works*, Charlestown, 1867.

3 Foothold

The Lord, whose promises are large to His Zion, *hath blessed his people's provision, and satisfied her poor with bread.* In a very little while everything in the country proved a staple commodity—wheat, rye, oats, barley, beef, pork, fish, butter, cheese, timber, mast, tar, rope, plankboard frames of houses, clapboard, and pipe-staves. And those who were formerly forced to fetch most of the bread they eat and beer they drink a hundred leagues by sea, have not only fed their elder sisters, Virginia, Barbadoes, and many of the Summer Islands (that were preferred for fruitfulness) but also the grandmother of us all, even the fertile Isle of Great Britain. Beside, Portugal hath had many a mouthful of bread and fish for us, in exchange for their Madeira liquor, and also Spain.

Nor could it be imagined that this wilderness should turn a mart for merchants in so short a space—Holland, France, Spain, and Portugal coming hither for trade, shipping going on gallantly.

Many a fair ship had her framing and finishing here, besides lesser vessels, barques, and ketches. Many a master, besides common seamen, had their first learning in this colony. All other trades have here fallen into their ranks and places, to their great advantage; especially coopers and shoemakers, enriching themselves by their trades very much. Carpenters, joiners, glaziers, painters follow their trades only. Gunsmiths, locksmiths, blacksmiths, nailors, cutlers have left the plow. Weavers, brewers, bakers, costermongers, feltmakers, braziers, pewterers and tinkers, rope-makers, masons, lime, brick, and tile-makers, cardmakers—to work and not to play. Turners, pumpmakers and wheelers, glovers, fellmongers and furriers, are orderly turned to their trades, besides divers sorts of shopkeepers, and some who have a mystery beyond others, as have the vintners.

CAPTAIN EDWARD JOHNSON
Wonder-Working Providence of Sion's Saviour, London, 1654.

Boston, being the center town and metropolis of this wilderness work, invironed as it is with the brinish floods, having one small isthmus which gives free acess to the neighbor towns, two constant fairs are kept for daily traffic thereunto.

The form of this town is like a heart, having two hills next to the sea. Betwixt these two strong arms lies a large cove or bay, on which the chiefest part of this town is built, overtopped with a third hill. All three, like overtopping towers, keep a constant watch to foresee the approach of foreign dangers, being furnished with a beacon and loud-babbling guns to give notice by their redoubled echo to all their sister towns.

This city-like town is crowded on the sea-banks, and wharfed out with great industry and cost. The buildings beautiful and large, and orderly placed with comely streets, whose continual enlargement presages some sumptuous city.

The wonder of this modern age!—that a few years should bring forth such great matters by so mean a handful! Behold the admirable acts of Christ: at this his people's landing, the hideous thickets in this place were such that wolves and bears nursed up their young from the eyes of all beholders—in those very places where the streets are full of boys and girls sporting up and down, with a continued concourse of people!

CAPTAIN EDWARD JOHNSON
Wonder-Working Providence of Sion's Saviour, London, 1654.

Foothold

SCHOOLS

To the end that learning may not be buried in the graves of our forefathers, in church and commonwealth, the Lord assisting our endeavors:

It is therefore ordered by the Court and authority thereof: that every township within this jurisdiction, after the Lord hath increased them to the number of fifty householders, shall then forthwith appoint one within their town to teach all such children as shall resort to him to write and read.

ALPHABET

A	In *Adam's* fall we sinned all.	N	*Noah* did view the old world and new.
B	Heaven to find the *Bible* mind.	O	Young *Obadias*, David, Josias, all were pious.
C	*Christ* crucified for sinners died.	P	*Peter* denied his Lord and cried.
D	The *Deluge* drowned the earth around.	Q	*Queen* Esther sues and saves the Jews.
E	*Elijah* hid by ravens fed.	R	Young pious *Ruth* left all for truth.
F	The Judgment made *Felix* afraid.	S	Young *Samuel* dear the Lord did fear.
G	As runs the *Glass* man's life doth pass.	T	Young *Timothy* learned sin to fly.
H	My Book and *Heart* shall never part.	V	*Vashti* for pride was set aside.
J	*Job* feels the rod yet blesses God.	W	*Whales* in the sea God's voice obey.
K	Proud *Korah's* troop was swallowed up.	X	*Xerxes* did die and so must I.
L	*Lot* fled to Zoar. Saw fiery shower on Sodom pour.	Y	While *Youth* doth cheer death may be near.
M	*Moses* was he who Israel's host led through the sea.	Z	*Zaccheus* he did climb the tree his Lord to see.

The General Laws and Liberties of the Massachusetts Colony, c. 1648.

New England Primer Improved, Boston, 1762.

Night of Prayer Among the Indians

Wuddtuckqunash, Ponamauta: *Let us lay on wood.*

This they do plentifully when they lie down to sleep winter and summer. Abundance they have and abundance they lay on; their fire is instead of our bedclothes. And so, themselves, and any that have occasion to lodge with them, must be content to turn often to the fire if the night be cold, and they who first wake must repair the fire.

Mauataunamoke: *Mend the fire.*

Nummattaquomen: *I have had a bad dream.*

When they have had a bad dream, which they conceive to be a threatening from God, they fall to prayer at all times of the night, especially before day.

I once travelled to an island of the wildest in our parts, where in the night an Indian had a vision or dream of the sun, whom they worship for a god, darting a beam into his breast, which he conceived to be the messenger of his death. This poor native called his friends and neighbors, and prepared some little refreshing for them, but himself was kept waking and fasting in great humiliations and invocations for ten days and nights.

I was alone, having travelled from my barque, the wind being contrary, and little could I speak to their understanding, especially because of the change in their dialect or manner of speech from our neighbors. Yet so much, through the help of God, I did speak, of the true and living only wise God, of the Creation, of Man and his fall from God, and so on, that at parting many burst forth, *Oh when will you come again, to bring us some more news of this God?*

God gives them sleep on ground, on straw, on sedgy mats or board,
When English softest beds of down sometimes no sleep afford.

I have known them leave their house and mat to lodge a friend or stranger,
When Jews and Christians oft have sent Christ Jesus to the manger.

'Fore day they invocate their gods, though many, false, and new:
O how should that God worshipped be who is but one and true?

THE REVEREND ROGER WILLIAMS
A Key into the Language of America, London, 1643.

BIRDS AND BEASTS

The Humbird is one of the wonders of the country, being no bigger than a hornet, yet hath all the dimensions of a bird, a bill and wings, with quills, spider-like legs, small claws; for colors, she is glorious as the rainbow; as she flies she makes a little humming noise like a humble-bee; wherefore she is called the Humbird.

The Pigeon of that country is something different from our dove-house pigeons in England; they have long tails like a magpie. These come into the country to go to the north parts in the beginning of our spring, at which time (if I may be counted worthy to be believed in a thing that is not so strange as true) I have seen them fly as if the airy regiment had been pigeons, seeing neither beginning nor ending, length nor breadth of these millions. The shouting of people, the rattling of guns, and pelting of small shot could not drive them out of their course, but so they continued for four or five hours together. Many of them build among the pine trees, thirty miles to the north-east of our plantations; joining nest to nest and tree to tree by their nests, so that the sun never sees the ground in that place, from whence the Indians fetch whole loads of them.

The Turkey is a very large bird of a black color, yet white in flesh; much bigger than our English turkey. He hath the use of his long legs so ready that he can run as fast as a dog, and fly as well as a goose; of these sometimes there will be forty, three-score, and a hundred in a flock, sometimes more and sometimes less; their feeding is acorns, hawes and berries, some of them get a haunt to frequent English corn. In winter when the snow covers the ground, they resort to the sea-shore to look for shrimps, and such small fishes at low tides. Such as love turkey hunting must follow it in winter after a new fallen snow, when he may follow them by their tracks. These turkeys remain all the year long; the price of a good turkey cock is four shillings; and he is well worth it, for he may be in weight forty pounds.

For Bears they be common, being a black kind of bear, which be most fierce in strawberry time, at which time they have young ones; at which time likewise they will go upright like a man, and climb trees, and swim to the islands, which if the Indians see, there will be more sportful bear-baiting than Paris garden can afford. For seeing the bears take water, an Indian will leap after him, where they go to water cuffs for bloody noses, and scratched sides; in the end the man gets the victory, riding the bear over the watery plain till he can bear him no longer. In the winter they take themselves to the cliffs of the rocks and thick swamps, to shelter them from the cold; and food being scant in those cold and hard times, they live only by sleeping and sucking their paws, which keepeth them as fat as they are in summer. They never prey upon the English cattle, or offer to assault the person of any man, unless being vexed with a shot and a man run upon them before they are dead, in which case they will stand in their own defence.

The Porcupine is a small thing not much unlike a hedge-hog; who stands upon his guard, and proclaims a *Noli me tangere* to man and beast that shall approach too near him, darting his quills into the legs and sides.

The Racoon is a deep furred beast, not much unlike a badger, having a tail like a fox, as good meat as a lamb. These beasts in the day time sleep in hollow trees; in the moonshine night they go to feed on clams at a low tide, by the sea side, where the English hunt them with their dogs.

WILLIAM WOOD
New England's Prospect, London, 1639.

Foothold

After God had carried us safe to New England, and we had builded our houses, provided necessaries for our livelihood, reared convenient places for God's worship, and settled the civil government: One of the next things we longed for, and looked after was how to advance learning and perpetuate it to Posterity; dreading to leave an illiterate ministry to the churches, when our present ministers shall lie in the dust.

And as we were thinking and consulting how to effect this great work, it pleased God to stir up the heart of one Mr Harvard (a godly gentleman, and a lover of learning, there living amongst us) to give the one half of his estate (it being in all about £1700) towards the erecting of a college: and all his library. After him another gave £300, others after them cast in more, and the public hand of the State added the rest. The college was, by common consent, appointed to be at Cambridge (a place very pleasant and accommodate), and is called (according to the name of the first founder) *Harvard College*.

New England's First Fruits, London, 1643.

CIVIL POWER

I infer that the sovereign, original, and foundation of civil power lies in the people. And if so, that a people may erect and establish what form of government seems to them most meet for their civil condition. It is evident that such governments as are by them erected and established have no more power, nor for no longer time, than the civil power, or people consenting and agreeing shall betrust them with. This is clear not only in reason but in the experience of all common-weales, where the people are not deprived of their natural freedom by the power of tyrants.

THE REVEREND ROGER WILLIAMS
Preface, *The Bloody Tenent of Persecution for Cause of Conscience*, London, 1644.

4 Quakers

WARNING TO HERETICS AND LIBERTINES

All who intend to transport themselves hither may know that this is no place of licentious liberty, nor will this people suffer any to trample down the Vineyard of the Lord, but with diligent execution will cut off from the City of the Lord the wicked doers. For it is not wrong to any man that a people who have spent their estates, many of them, and ventured their lives, to keep faith and a pure conscience, to use all means that the Word of God allows for maintenance and continuance of the same, especially [if] they have taken up a desolate wilderness for their habitation. If any will yet, notwithstanding, seek to jostle them out of their right, let them not wonder if they meet with all the opposition a people put to their greatest straits can make.

CAPTAIN EDWARD JOHNSON
Wonder-Working Providence of Sion's Saviour, London, 1654.

The Whipping of the Quakers

At Dover, dated December 22, 1662

To the constables of Dover, Hampton, Salisbury, Newbury, Rowley, Ipswich, Lynn, Boston, Roxbury, Dedham, and until these Vagabond-Quakers are carried out of this jurisdiction:

You, and every one of you, are required in the King's Majesty's Name, to take the Vagabond-Quakers, Ann Coleman, Mary Tompkins, Alice Ambrose, and make them fast to the cart's tail, and driving the cart through your several towns, to whip them on their backs, not exceeding ten stripes apiece in each town, and so convey them from constable to constable till they come out of this jurisdiction, as you will answer it at your peril; and this shall be your warrant.

Per me,
Richard Walden

So, on a very cold day, your deputy, Walden, caused these women to be stripped from the middle upward, and tied to a cart, and after a while cruelly whipped them; which some of their friends seeing testified against, for which Walden put two of them in the stocks. Having despatched them in this town, [Walden] made way to carry them over the waters and through the woods to another. The women denied to go unless they had a copy of their warrant. So your executioner sought to set them on horseback, but they slid off. Then they endeavored to tie each to a man on horseback; that would not do either, nor any course they took, till the copy was given them; insomuch that he was almost wearied with them. But the copy being given them, they went with the executioner.

And through dirt and snow at Salisbury, halfway the leg deep, the constable forced them after the cart's tail, at which he whipped them. Under which cruelty and sore usage, the tender women traversing their way through all was a hard spectacle to those who had in them anything of tenderness. But the presence of the Lord was so with them, in the extremity of their sufferings, that they sung in the midst of them, to the astonishment of their enemies.

At Hampton, William Fifield, the constable, the next morning would have whipped them before day, but they refused, saying that they were not ashamed of their sufferings. Then he would have whipped them on their clothes, contrary to the warrant, when he had them at the cart. But they said, 'Set us free, or do according to thy order,' which was to whip them on their naked backs. Then he spake to a woman to take off their clothes. The woman said she would not do it for all the world, and so did other women deny to do it. Then he said, 'I profess, I will do it myself.' So he stripped them, and then stood trembling, with the whip in his hand, as a man condemned, and did the execution in that condition.

Now, amongst the rest of the spectators, Edward Wharton, beholding their torn bodies and weary steps, and yet no remorse in their persecutors, could not withhold, but testified against them, seeing this bloody engagement. Whereupon one of your officers said, 'Edward Wharton, what do you here?'

'I am here,' answered Edward, 'to see your wickedness and cruelty, that so if you kill them, I may be able to declare how you murdered them.'

But the Lord unexpectedly wrought a way at that time to deliver them out of the tyrants' hands, so through three towns only were they whipped, but cruelly, and then they were discharged.

GEORGE BISHOP
New England Judged by the Spirit of the Lord, London, 1703.

Lydia Wardel Goes to Newbury Church as a Sign

Lydia, being a young and tender chaste woman, feeling the wickedness of your priests and rulers to her husband, withdrew and separated from your church at Newbury. She had been often sent for to come thither to give a reason of such her separation. In the consideration of their miserable condition, who were thus blinded with ignorance and persecution, as a sign to them she went in naked amongst them, though it was exceeding hard to her modest and shamefaced disposition.

Which put them into such a rage, instead of consideration, that they soon laid hand on her. And to the next court at Ipswich had her, where, without law, they condemned her to be tied to the fence-post of the tavern—which is usually their court-places, where they may serve their ears with music and their bellies with wine and gluttony. Whereunto she was tied, stripped from the waist upwards, with her naked breasts to the splinters of the posts, and there sorely lashed with twenty or thirty cruel stripes. Which though it miserably tore and bruised her tender body, yet to the joy of her husband and friends that were spectators, she was carried through all these inhumane cruelties quiet and cheerful, to the shame and confusion of these unreasonable men, whose names shall rot and their memory perish.

The Hanging of the Quaker William Leddra

On the 14th of this instant, here was one William Leddra, which was put to death. I am not of his opinion, but yet truly methought the Lord did mightily appear in the man.

I went to one of the magistrates of Cambridge, who had been on the jury that condemned him, and I asked him by what rule he did it? He answered me that he was a rogue, a very rogue. 'But what is this to the question?' I said. 'What is your rule?' He answered, 'He had abused authority.'

Then I goes after the man William Leddra, and asked him, 'Whether he did not look on it as a breach of rule, to slight and undervalue authority?' when the man was on the ladder. He looked on me and called me friend, and said, 'Know that this day I am willing to offer up my life for the witness of Jesus.'

Then I desired leave of the officers to speak, and said, 'Gentlemen, I am a stranger both to your persons and country, and yet a friend to both.' And I cried aloud, *'For the Lord's sake, take not away the man's life, but remember Gamaliel's counsel to the Jews: If this be of man, it will come to nought, but if it be of God, ye cannot overthrow it. Be careful ye be not found fighters against God.'*

GEORGE BISHOP
New England Judged by the Spirit of the Lord, London, 1703.

THOMAS WILKIE
From a letter quoted by George Bishop in *New England Judged by the Spirit of the Lord*, London, 1703.

The Bloody Tenent

The Doctrine of Persecution for cause of conscience is proved guilty of all the blood of the souls crying for vengeance under the altar.

It is the will and command of God that, since the coming of his Son, the Lord Jesus, a permission of the most paganish, Jewish, Turkish, or Anti-Christian consciences and worships be granted to all men in all nations; and they are only to be fought against with that sword which is only, in soul matters, able to conquer—to wit, the sword of God's Spirit, the Word of God.

God requireth not an uniformity of religion to be inacted and inforced in any civil state; which inforced uniformity sooner or later is the greatest occasion of civil war, ravishing of conscience, persecution of Christ Jesus in his servants, and of the hypocrisy and destruction of millions of souls.

THE REVEREND ROGER WILLIAMS
Preface, *The Bloody Tenent of Persecution for Cause of Conscience*, London, 1644.

5 Savages

Pursuit

In this March, they came to an Indian town, where there were many wigwams in sight, but an icy swamp prevented their running at once upon it. There was much firing upon each side. But at length the enemy all fled, and a certain Mohegan that was a friend Indian, pursued and seized one of the enemy that had a small wound in his leg, and brought him before the General, where he was examined. Some were for torturing him to a more ample confession of what he knew concerning his country men. Mr Church, verily believing he had been ingenuous in his confession, interceded, and prevailed for his escaping torture. But the army being bound forward in its march, and the Indian's wound somewhat disenabling him for travelling, it was concluded he should be knocked on the head. Accordingly, he was brought before a great fire, and the Mohegan that took him was allowed, as he desired to be, the executioner.

Mr Church, taking no delight in the sport, framed an errand at some distance among the baggage horses. And when he had got some ten rods, or thereabouts, from the fire, the executioner fetching a blow with his hatchet at the head of the prisoner, he dodged his head aside, and the executioner missing his stroke, the hatchet flew out of his hand and had like to have done execution where it was not designed.

The prisoner broke from them that held him, and notwithstanding his wound, made use of his legs, and happened to run right upon Mr Church, who laid hold on him, and a close scuffle they had. But the Indian having no clothes slipped from him and ran again. And Mr Church pursued, until the Indian stumbled and fell, and they closed again—scuffled and fought pretty smartly, until the Indian, by the advantage of his nakedness, slipped from his hold again, and set on his third race, with Mr Church close at his heels, endeavoring to lay hold on the hair of his head, which was all the hold could be taken of him. And running through a swamp that was covered with hollow ice, it made so loud a noise that Mr Church expected that some of his English friends would follow the noise and come to his assistance.

The Indian happened to run athwart a mighty tree that lay fallen near breast high, where he stopped and cried aloud for help. But Mr Church being soon upon him again, the Indian seized him fast by the hair of his head, and endeavored by twisting to break his neck. But though Mr Church's wounds had somewhat weakened him, and the Indian a stout fellow, yet he held him well in play and twisted the Indian's neck as well, and took advantage of many opportunities, while they hung by each other's hair, to give him notorious bunts in the face with his head.

In the heat of the scuffle they heard the ice break with somebody's coming apace to them. Church concluded there was help for one or other of them, but was doubtful which of them must now receive the fatal stroke. Anon somebody comes up to them, who proved to be the Indian that had first taken the prisoner. Without speaking a word he felt them out (for it was so dark he could not distinguish them by sight, the one being clothed and the other naked), he felt where Mr Church's hands were fastened in the Netop's hair and with one blow settled his hatchet between them, and ended the strife.

He then spoke to Mr Church and hugged him in his arms, and thanked him abundantly for catching the prisoner, and cut off the head of the victim and carried it to the camp, and giving an account to the rest of the friend Indians in the camp how Mr Church has seized his prisoner, they all joined in a mighty shout.

THOMAS CHURCH
The Entertaining History of King Philip's War, ... with some account of the Divine Providence toward Col. Benjamin Church, Boston, 1716.

THE BURNING OF LANCASTER

On the 10th of February, 1676, came the Indians with great numbers upon Lancaster. The first coming was about sun-rising. Hearing the noise of some guns we looked out; several houses were burning and the smoke ascending to heaven.

They came and beset our house, and quickly it was the dolefullest day that ever mine eyes saw. Some of the Indians got behind the hill, others into the barn, and others behind anything that would shelter them; from all which places they shot against the house so that the bullets seemed to fly like hail. And quickly they wounded one man among us, then another, then a third. About two hours (according to my observation in that amazing time) they had been about the house before they prevailed to fire it, which they did with flax and hemp which they brought from the barn. And one ventured out and quenched it, but they quickly fired it again and that took.

Now is the dreadful hour come that I have often heard of, but now mine eyes see it. Then I took my children to go forth and leave the house, but as soon as we came to the door and appeared, the Indians shot so thick that the bullets rattled against the house as if one had taken a handful of stones and threw them, so that we were forced to give back. We had six stout dogs belonging to the garrison, but none of them would stir, though at another time if an Indian had come to the door, they were ready to fly upon him and tear him down.

But out we must go, the fire increasing and coming along behind us roaring, and the Indians gaping before us with their guns, spears, and hatchets to devour us. No sooner were we out of the house but my brother-in-law, being before wounded in defending the house, in or near the throat, fell down dead, whereat the Indians scornfully shouted and hallooed, and were presently upon him, stripping off his clothes.

The bullets flying thick, one went through my side, and the same, as it would seem, through the bowels and hand of my poor child in my arms. One of my elder sister's children, named William, had then his leg broke, which the Indians perceiving they knocked him on the head. Thus were we butchered by these merciless heathens, standing amazed with the blood running down to our heels. My eldest sister, being yet in the house, and seeing these woful sights, the infidels hauling mothers one way and children another, and her eldest son telling her that William was dead, and myself was wounded, she said. 'And, Lord, let me die with them,' which was no sooner said but she was struck with a bullet and fell down dead over the threshold.

Come, behold the works of the Lord, what desolations he hath made in the earth. Of thirty-seven persons who were in this one house, none escaped either present death or a bitter captivity save only one, who might say as in JOB, 'And I only am escaped alone to tell the news.' There was one who was chopped in the head with a hatchet, and stripped naked, and yet was crawling up and down. It was a solemn sight to see so many Christians lying in their bloods, some here and some there, like a company of sheep torn by wolves. All of them stripped naked by a company of hellhounds, roaring, singing, ranting, and insulting, as if they would have torn our very hearts out. Yet the Lord, by his almighty power, preserved a number of us from death, for there were twenty-four of us taken alive and carried captive.

MARY ROWLANDSON
The Sovereignty and Goodness of God: a narrative of the captivity and restoration of Mrs. Mary Rowlandson, Cambridge, 1682.

HANNAH DUSTAN

On March 15, 1697, the savages made a descent upon the skirts of Haverhill, murdering and captiving about thirty-nine persons, and burning about half a dozen houses. In this broil, one Hannah Dustan, having lain-in about a week, attended with her nurse, Mary Neff, a widow, a body of terrible Indians drew near unto the house.

Her husband hastened from his employments abroad and, first bidding seven of his eight children, which were from two to seventeen years of age, to get away as fast as they could unto some garrison in the town, he went in to inform his wife of the horrible distress come upon them. Ere she could get up, the fierce Indians were got so near that, utterly despairing to do her any service, he ran out after his children; resolving that, on the horse which he had with him, he would ride away with that which he should in this extremity find his affections to pitch most upon, and leave the rest unto the care of the Divine Providence.

He overtook his children about forty rod from his door, but then such was the agony of his parental affections, that he found it impossible for him to distinguish any one of them from the rest; wherefore he took up a courageous resolution to live and die with them all. A party of Indians came up with him, and now though they fired at him, and he fired at them, yet he manfully kept at the rear of his little army of unarmed children, while they marched off with the pace of a child of five years old, until, by the singular providence of God, he arrived with them all unto a place of safety about a mile or two from his house.

But his house must, in the meantime, have more dismal tragedies enacted at it. The nurse, trying to escape with the new-born infant, fell into the hands of the formidable savages. And those furious tawnies, coming into the house, bid poor Dustan to rise immediately. Full of astonishment she did so; and sitting down in the chimney with an heart full of most fearful expectation, she saw the raging dragons rifle all that they could carry away, and set the house on fire.

About nineteen or twenty Indians now led these away, with about half a score other English captives; but ere they had gone many steps, they dashed out the brains of the infant against a tree, and several other captives, as they began to tire in their sad journey, were soon sent unto their long home: the savages would presently bury their hatchets in their brains and leave their carcasses on the ground for birds and beasts to feed upon.

However, Dustan, with her nurse, notwithstanding her present condition, travelled that night about a dozen miles, and then kept up with their new masters in a long travel of an hundred and fifty miles, more or less, without any sensible damage in their health, from the hardships of their travel, their lodging, their diet, and their many other difficulties.

Their Indian master sometimes, when he saw them dejected, would say unto them, 'What need you trouble yourself? If your God will have you delivered, you shall be so!' And it seems our God would have it so to be.

This Indian family was now travelling with these two captive women, and an English youth taken from Worcester a year and a half before, unto a rendezvous of savages, which they call a town, somewhere beyond Penacook. And they still told these poor women that when they came to this town they must be stript, and scourged, and run the gantlet through the whole army of Indians. They said this was the fashion when the captives first came to a town, and they derided some of the faint-hearted

English, which, they said, fainted and swooned away under the torments of this discipline.

But on April 30, while they were yet about a hundred and fifty miles from the Indian town, a little before break of day, when the whole crew was in a *dead sleep* (Reader, see if it prove not so!) one of these women took up a resolution to imitate the action of Jael upon Sisera, and, being where she had not her own life secured by any law, to take away the life of the murderers by whom her child had been butchered.

She heartened the nurse and the youth to assist her in this enterprise, and, all furnishing themselves with hatchets for the purpose, they struck such home blows upon the heads of their sleeping oppressors that, ere they could any of them struggle into any effectual resistance, at the feet of these poor prisoners they bowed, there they fell down dead.

Only one squaw escaped, sorely wounded, from them in the dark; and one boy, whom they reserved asleep, intending to bring him away with them, suddenly waked and scuttled away from this desolation.

But, cutting off the scalps of these ten wretches, they came off, and received fifty pounds from the General Assembly of the Province as a recompense of their action; besides which they received many presents of congratulation from their more private friends.

THE REVEREND COTTON MATHER
Magnalia Christi Americana, London, 1702.

6   *Heaven and Hell*

The Meekness of John Cotton

Once an humorous and imperious brother, following Mr Cotton home to his house after his public labors, rudely told him that his ministry was become generally either dark or flat. Whereto this meek man, very mildly and gravely, made only this answer: 'Both, brother, it may be, both. Let me have your prayers that it may be otherwise.' It is remarkable that the man thus sick afterwards died of those damnable heresies for which he was deservedly excommunicated.

Another time, when Mr Cotton had modestly replied unto one that would much talk and crack of his insight into the revelations: 'Brother, I must confess myself to want light in those mysteries,' the man went home and sent him *a pound of candles;* upon which this good man bestowed only a silent smile. He would not set the beacon of his great soul on fire at the landing of such a little cockboat.

I think I may not omit a remarkable passage which that good man, Mr Flavel, reports in a sermon on gospel unity:

'A company of vain, wicked men, having inflamed their blood in a tavern at Boston, and seeing that reverend, meek and holy minister of Christ, Mr Cotton, coming along the street, one of them tells his companions, "I'll go," saith he, and "put a trick on old Cotton."

'Down he goes, and crossing his way, whispers these words into his ear: "Cotton," saith he, "thou art an old fool."

'Mr Cotton replied, "I confess I am so; the Lord make both me and thee wiser, even wise unto salvation."

'He relates this message to his wicked companions, which cast a great damp upon their sports, in the midst of a frolic.'

THE REVEREND COTTON MATHER
Magnalia Christi Americana, London, 1702.

Heaven and Hell

MEMOIR: I am The Rose of Sharon and the Lily of the Valleys

The words seemed to me sweetly to represent the loveliness and beauty of Jesus Christ. The whole book of Canticles used to be pleasant to me, and I used to be much in reading it; and found, from time to time, an inward sweetness that would carry me away in my contemplations; and sometimes a kind of vision, of being alone in the mountains, or some solitary wilderness, sweetly conversing with Christ, and wrapt and swallowed up in God.

Not long after I first began to experience these things, I gave an account to my father of some things that had passed in my mind. I was pretty much affected by the discourse we had together; and when the discourse was ended, I walked abroad alone, in a solitary place in my father's pasture. And as I was walking there, and looking upon the sky and clouds, there came into my mind so sweet a sense of the glorious *majesty* and *grace* of God as I know not how to express.—I seemed to see majesty and meekness joined together; it was a sweet, and gentle, and holy majesty; and also a majestic meekness, a high, and great, and holy gentleness.

After this my sense of divine things became more and more lively. The appearance of everything was altered; divine glory seemed to appear in everything; in the sun, moon, and stars, in the clouds and blue sky, in the grass, flowers, trees, in the water and all nature. I often used to sit and view the moon for a long time, and in the day spent much time in viewing the clouds and sky, to behold the sweet glory of God in these things. I used to be struck with terror when I saw a thunder-storm rising. But now, on the contrary, it rejoiced me. I felt God, if I may so speak, at the first appearance of a thunder-storm, and used at such times to fix myself in order to view the clouds and see the lightnings play. While thus engaged, it always seemed natural to me to chant forth my meditations with a singing voice.

THE REVEREND JONATHAN EDWARDS
Works, New York, 1829-30, vol. I.

SERMON: The Eternity of Hell Torments

Be entreated to consider attentively how great and awful a thing eternity is.

Do but consider what it is to suffer extreme torment forever and ever; to suffer it day and night, from one day to another, from one year to another, from one age to another, from one thousand ages to another, and so, adding age to age, and thousands to thousands, in pain, in wailing and lamenting, groaning and shrieking and gnashing your teeth, with your souls full of dreadful grief and amazement, with your bodies and every member full of racking torture, without any possibility of getting ease; without any possibility of moving God to pity by your cries; without any possibility of diverting your thoughts from your pain; without any possibility of obtaining any manner of mitigation, or help, or change for the better any way.

Do but consider how dreadful despair will be in such torment. To have no hope; when you shall wish that you might be turned into nothing, but shall have no hope of it; when you shall wish that you might be turned into a toad or a serpent, but shall have no hope of it; when you would rejoice, if you might but have any relief, after you shall have endured these torments millions of ages, but shall have no hope of it; when, after you shall have worn out the age of the sun, moon, and stars in your dolorous groans and lamentations, without any rest day or night, or one minute's ease, yet you shall have no hope of ever being delivered, but shall know that you are not one whit nearer the end of your torments; but that still there are the same groans, the same shrieks, the same doleful cries incessantly to be made by you and the smoke of your torment shall still ascend up, forever and ever; and that your soul, which shall have been agitated with the wrath of God all this while, yet will still exist to bear more wrath; your bodies, which shall have been burning all this while in these glowing flames, yet shall not have been consumed.

THE REVEREND JONATHAN EDWARDS
Sermon XI, *Works,* New York, 1829-30, vol. VI.

DIARY

January 13, 1695/6.

When I came in, past seven at night, my wife met me in the entry and told me Betty had surprised them. It seems Betty had given some signs of dejection and sorrow; a little after dinner she burst into an amazing cry, which caused all the family to cry too. Her mother asked her the reason; she gave none. At last she said she was afraid she should go to hell, her sins were not pardoned. She was first wounded by my reading a sermon of Mr Norton's, text: *Ye shall seek me and shall not find me.* And these words in the sermon, *Ye shall seek me and shall die in your sins,* ran in her mind and terrified her greatly. And staying home she read out of Mr Cotton Mather, *Why hath Satan filled thy heart?* which increased her fear. Her mother asked her whether she prayed. She answered yes, but feared her prayers were not heard because her sins not pardoned.

Mr Willard—though sent for timelier, yet not been told of the message—came not till after I came home. He discoursed with Betty, who could not give a distinct account, but was confused. Mr Willard prayed excellently. The Lord bring light and comfort out of this dark and dreadful cloud, and grant that Christ's being formed in my dear child may be the issue of these dreadful pangs.

JUDGE SAMUEL SEWALL
Diary, 1878-82.

MASSACHUSETTS LAWS

Sabbath, 1653

Upon information of sundry abuses and misdemeanors committed by divers persons on the Lord's day, not only in children playing in the streets and other places, but by youths, maids, and other persons, both strangers and others, uncivilly walking in the streets and fields, travelling from town to town, going on shipboard, frequenting common-houses and other places to drink, sport, or otherwise to mispend that precious time,

It is therefore ordered by this Court and the Authority thereof: that no children, youths, maids or other persons shall transgress in the like kind, on penalty of being reputed great provokers of the high displeasure of Almighty God; and further incur the penalty hereafter expressed, viz: For the first offence, be admonished; for a second offence, shall pay as a fine five shillings, and for the third offence, ten shillings. And if any be unable or unwilling to pay the aforesaid fines, they shall be whipped by the Constable, not exceeding five stripes for ten shillings fine.

Provoking Evils

Whereas there is manifest pride openly appearing amongst us, in that long hair like women's hair is worn by some men, either their own or others' made into periwigs, and by some women cutting, curling, and immodest laying out their hair, which practice doth prevail and increase especially among the younger sort; the evil of pride in apparel, both for costliness in the poorer sort, and vain, new, strange fashions both in poor and rich, with naked breasts and arms, pinioned with the addition of superfluous ribbons both on hair and apparel:

For redress thereof, it is ordered by this Court that the County Courts give strict charge to present all such persons and shall impose a fine upon them at their discretion.

Whereas there is a loose and sinful custom of going or riding from town to town, and that oft times men and women together, upon pretence of going to lectures, but it appears merely to drink and revel in ordinaries and taverns, which is in itself scandalous, and it is to be feared a notable means to debauch our youth, and hazard the chastity of such as are drawn thereunto:

For prevention thereof: it is ordered by this Court that all single persons who merely for their pleasure take such journeys, shall be reputed and accounted riotous and unsober and shall be liable to be summoned to appear any County Court, Magistrate or Commissioner; and being convicted thereof, shall give bond for their good behavior twenty pounds, and upon refusal so to do, shall be committed to prison for ten days.

Penalty for drinking healths &c. in ships or vessels, 1663

Be it enacted by the Authority of this Court: that no masters of ships, or seamen, having their vessels riding within any of our harbors shall presume to drink healths, or suffer healths to be drunk within their vessels by day or by night, or to shoot off any gun after the daylight is past or on the Sabbath day, on penalty for every health twenty shillings and for every gun so shot twenty shillings.

Scolds

Whereas there is no expressed punishment affixed to the evil practice of sundry persons by exorbitancy of the tongue, in railing or scolding,

It is therefore ordered: that all such persons convicted before any Court or Magistrate shall be gagged, or set in a ducking stool and dipt over head and ears in some convenient place of fresh or salt water.

The General Laws and Liberties of the Massachusetts Colony, Cambridge, 1672.

Heaven and Hell

Fined, March, 1657:

John Hathorne, for suffering persons to sit tippling in his house and at several times to be drunk. Oliver Purchis and George Darline, both at the Iron Works, deposed that in February last, in the moonlight, they went to Lynn town to the ordinary. They found a great store in the house drinking. Sargeant Eldridge of Malden, who had been there the greater part of the day before, slept by the fire all night, and if deponent had not been there, his clothes and perhaps himself would have been burned. In one room was one Muzzy and his wife, she sitting on one side of the table between two men and her husband on the other merrily singing to the rest.

Whipped, September, 1656:

Evin Moris of Topsfield, for reviling the ordinance of God and such as are in the church fellowship, saying that when some was together keeping a day of humiliation that they were howling like wolves and lifting up their paws for their children, and if there had been no members of churches, there would have been no need of gallows.

Records of the Quarterly Court of Essex County, Massachusetts, vol. II, 1656-62.

7 Witchcraft

Plague of Evil Angels

An Army of Devils is horribly broken in upon the place which is the center, and, after a sort, the first-born of our English settlements. And the houses of the good people there are filled with the doleful shrieks of their children and servants, tormented by invisible hands, with tortures altogether preternatural.

After the mischiefs there endeavored, and since in part conquered, the terrible plague of evil angels hath made its progress into some other places, where other persons have in like manner been diabolically handled. These our poor afflicted neighbors, quickly after they become infected and infested with these demons, arrive to a capacity of discerning the shapes of their troublers. And notwithstanding the great and just suspicion that the demons might impose the shapes of innocent persons in their spectral exhibition upon the sufferers (which may prove no small part of the witch-plot), yet many of the persons thus represented, being examined, have been convicted of a very damnable witchcraft. Yea, more than twenty have confessed that they have signed unto a book which the Devil showed them, and engaged in his hellish design of bewitching and ruining our land.

THE REVEREND COTTON MATHER
The Wonders of the Invisible World, Boston, 1692.

The Humble Declaration of Margaret Jacobs unto the Honored Court now sitting at Salem showeth that, whereas your poor and humble declarant being closely confined here in Salem jail for the crime of witchcraft—which crime, thanks be to the Lord! I am altogether ignorant of, as will appear at the great day of judgment,—I was cried out upon by some of the possessed persons as afflicting them. Whereupon I was brought to examination, which persons at the sight of me fell down, which did very much startle and affright me. The Lord above knows I knew nothing in the least measure how or who afflicted them. They told me, Without doubt I did, or else they would not fall down at me. They told me, If I would not confess, I should be put down into the dungeon and would be hanged, but, if I did confess, I should have my life. My vile, wicked heart, to save my life, made me make the confession I did. Which confession, may it please the honored Court, is altogether untrue.

The very first night after I made confession, I was in such horror of conscience that I could not sleep, for fear the Devil should carry me away for telling such horrid lies. What I said was altogether false against my grandfather and Mr Burroughs* which I did to save my life and to have my liberty. But the Lord charging it to my conscience, I could not contain myself before I had denied my confession, though I saw nothing but death before me, choosing rather death with a quiet conscience than to live in such horror. Whereupon I was committed to close prison, where I have enjoyed more felicity in spirit a thousand times than I did before in my enlargement. And now your declarant do leave it to Your Honors' pious and judicious discretion to take pity on my young and tender years, to act and do with me as the Lord above and Your Honors shall see good, having no friends but the Lord to plead my cause for me. And your poor and humble declarant shall forever pray for Your Honors' happiness in this life and eternal felicity in the world to come.

*Both of whom were among the 19 hanged on August 19, 1692, despite this confession.

MARGARET JACOBS

We whose names are underwritten, being in the year 1692 called to serve as jurors in court at Salem on trial of many who were by some suspected of witchcraft:

We confess that we were not capable to understand, nor able to withstand, the mysterious delusions of the powers of darkness and prince of the air; but were, for want of knowledge in ourselves, and better information from others, prevailed with to take up such evidence against the accused as we justly fear was insufficient for touching the lives of any. Whereby we fear we have been instrumental, with others, though ignorantly and unwillingly, to bring upon ourselves and this people of the Lord the guilt of innocent blood.

We do therefore hereby signify to all in general, and to the surviving sufferers in especial, our deep sense of and sorrow for our errors; for which we are much disquieted and distressed in our minds; and do therefore humbly beg forgiveness of God for Christ's sake, and we also pray that we may be considered candidly and aright by the living sufferers as being then under the power of a strong and general delusion.

We do heartily ask forgiveness of you all, whom we have justly offended; and do declare we would none of us do such things again for the whole world; praying you to accept of this in way of satisfaction for our offense; and that you would bless the inheritance of the Lord, that he may be entreated for the land.

Foreman Thomas Fisk, William Fisk, John Batcheller, Thomas Fisk, Jun., John Dane, Joseph Eveleth, Thomas Pearley, Sen., John Peabody, Thomas Perkins, Samuel Sayer, Andrew Elliot, Henry Werrick, Sen.

Quoted by Robert Calef in *More Wonders of the Invisible World*, London, 1700.

PART TWO

I *Native Earth*

NEWBURY

As long as Plum Island shall faithfully keep the commanded post, notwithstanding all the hectoring words and hard blows of the proud and boisterous ocean; as long as any salmon or sturgeon shall swim in the streams of Merrimack; or any perch or pickerel in Crane Pond; as long as the sea-fowl shall know the time of their coming; as long as any cattle shall be fed with the grass growing in the meadows which do humbly bow themselves down before Turkey Hill; as long as any sheep shall walk upon Old Town Hills, and shall from thence pleasantly look down upon the River Parker; as long as any free and harmless doves shall find a white oak, or other tree within the township to perch, or feed, or build a careless nest upon; and shall voluntarily present themselves to perform the office of gleaners after barley harvest; as long as Nature shall not grow old and dote, but shall constantly remember to give the rows of Indian corn their education by pairs: so long shall Christians be born there.

JUDGE SAMUEL SEWALL
Phaenomena Quaedam Apocalyptica, Boston, 1727.

JOURNEY FROM BOSTON TO NEW YORK, 1704

In about an hour after we left the swamp, we came to Billing's, where I was to lodge. My guide very complacently helped me down and showed the door, signing me with his hand to go in; which I gladly did—but had not gone many steps into the room, ere I was interrogated by a young lady I understood afterwards was the eldest daughter of the family, viz: 'Law for me!—what in the world brings you here at this time of the night? I never see a woman on the road so dreadful late in all the days of my versal life. Who are you? Where you going? I'm scared out of my wits!'—with much more of the same kind. I stood aghast, preparing to reply, when in comes my guide. To him madam turned, roaring out: 'Lawful heart, John, it is you?—howdedoo! Where in the world are you going with this woman? Who is she?' John made no answer, but sat down in the corner, fumbled out his black junk, and saluted that instead of Deb.

Miss stared awhile, drew a chair, bade me sit, and then ran upstairs and put on two or three rings (or else I had not seen them before) and returning, set herself just before me, showing the way to Redding, that I might see her ornaments. But her granam's new rung sow, had it appeared, would have affected me as much. I paid honest John with money and dram according to contract, and dismissed him, and prayed Miss to show me where I must lodge. She conducted me to a parlor in a little back lean-to, almost filled with the bedstead, which was so high that I was forced to climb on a chair to get up to the wretched bed that lay on it; on which, having stretched my tired limbs, and laid my head on a sad-colored pillow, I began to think of the past day.

Tuesday, October 3.

The post told me we had near fourteen miles to ride to the next stage, where we were to lodge. I asked him of the road, foreseeing we must travel in the night. He told me there was a bad river, which was so very fierce a horse could sometimes hardly stem it; but it was but narrow, and we should soon be over. I cannot express the concern of mind this relation set me in, tormenting me with blackest ideas of my approaching fate, sometimes seeing myself drowning, otherwhiles drowned, and at the best like a holy sister just come out of a spiritual bath in dripping garments.

The only glimmering we now had was from the spangled skies. Each lifeless trunk, with its shattered limbs, appeared an armed enemey; and every little stump like a ravenous devourer. Nor could I so much as discern my guide, which added to my terror. Thus, absolutely lost in thoughts and dying with the very thoughts of dying, I came up with the post, whom I did not see till even with his horse. We entered a thicket of trees and shrubs, and I perceived by the horse's going we were on the descent of a hill, which as we came nearer the bottom, was totally dark. But I knew by the going of the horse we had entered the water. I now rallied all the courage I was mistress of, knowing I must either venture my fate of drowning, or be left like the children in the wood. So, as the post bid me, I gave reins to my nag; and in a few minutes got safe to the other side.

From hence we kept on with more ease than before, the way being smooth and even, the night warm and serene. The tall and thick trees, when the moon glared through the branches, filled my imagination with the pleasant delusions of a sumptuous city, with spiring steeples, balconies, galleries and I know not what, grandeurs which the stories of foreign countries had given me the idea of. Being thus agreeably entertained without a thought of anything but thoughts themselves, I on a sudden was roused by the post's sounding his horn, which assured me he was arrived at the stage where we were to lodge; and that music was then most musical and agreeable to me.

Being come to Mr Haven's, I was very civilly received, and courteously entertained in a clean, comfortable house; and the good woman was very active in helping off my riding clothes, and then asked what I would eat. I told her I had some chocolate, if she would prepare it; which, with the help of some milk and a little clean brass kettle she soon effected to my satisfaction. I then betook me to my apartment, a little room parted from the kitchen by a single board partition. After I had noted the occurrences of the day, I went to bed, which, though pretty hard, yet neat and handsome. But I could get no sleep, because of the clamor of some of the town topers in the next room, who were entered into a strong debate concerning the signification of the name of their country: viz. *Narragansett,* with such a roaring voice and thundering blows with the fist of wickedness on the table that it pierced my head. I heartily fretted and wished them tongue-tied. They kept calling for t'other gill, which while they were swallowing was some intermission, but presently like oil to fire increased the flame. I set my candle on a chest by the bedside, and sitting up, fell to my old way of composing my resentments:

I ask thy aid, O potent Rum!
To charm these wranging topers dumb.
Thou hast their giddy brains possest—
And I, poor I, can get no rest.
Intoxicate them with thy fumes;
O still their tongues till morning comes!

And I know not but my wishes took effect; for the dispute soon ended with t'other dram; and so good night!

Wednesday, October 4th.

About four in the morning we set out for Kingston. This road was poorly furnished with accommodations for travellers, so that we were forced to ride twenty-two miles by the post's account, but nearer thirty by mine, before we could bait so much as our horses. But the post encouraged me by saying we should be well accommodated at Mr Devil's a few miles further. I questioned whether we ought to go to the Devil to be helped out of affliction; however, like the rest of deluded souls that post to the infernal den, we made all possible speed to this devil's habitation. Where alighting, we were going in, but meeting his two daughters—as I supposed, twins, they so nearly resembled each other, and looked as old as the Devil himself and quite as ugly—we could hardly get a word out of them. Till, with our importunity, telling them our necessity, &c., they called the old sophister, who was as sparing of his word as his daughters had been, and 'No,' or 'None,' were the replies he made to our demands. He differed only in this from the old fellow in t'other country: he let us depart.

SARAH KEMBLE KNIGHT
Private Journal Kept on a Journey from Boston to New York in the Year 1704.

BUNDLING

Notwithstanding the modesty of the females is such that it would be accounted the greatest rudeness for a gentleman to speak before a lady of a garter, knee, or leg, yet it is thought but a piece of civility to ask her to *bundle*. It is certainly innocent, virtuous, and prudent, or the Puritans would never have permitted it to prevail. Children brought up with the chastest ideas—with so much religion as to believe the omniscient God sees them in the dark and that angels guide them while they sleep—will not, nay, cannot act a wicked thing. People who are influenced more by lust than a serious faith in God ought never to *bundle*. If any man, thus a stranger to the love of virtue, of God and the Christian religion, should *bundle* with a young lady in New England, and behave himself unseemly towards her, he must first melt her into passion, and expell heaven, death, and hell from her mind, or—if he escape with life, it will be owing to the parents flying from their bed to protect him.

The Indians, who had this method of courtship when the English arrived among them, are the most chaste set of people in the world. Concubinage and fornication are vices none of them are addicted to, except such as foresake the laws of Hobbamockow and turn Christians. The savages have taken many female prisoners, carried them back three hundred miles into their country, and kept them several years, and yet not a single instance of their violating the laws of chastity has ever been known. This cannot be said of the French, or of the English, whenever Indian or other women have fallen into their hands.

I am no advocate for temptation; yet must say that *bundling* has prevailed 160 years in New England, and, I verily believe, with ten times more chastity than the sitting on a sofa. I had daughters, and can speak from near forty years' experience. Bundling takes place only in the cold seasons of the year—the sofa in summer is more dangerous than the bed in winter. About 1756, Boston, Salem, Newport, and New York, resolving to be more polite than their ancestors, forbade their daughters bundling on the bed with any young men whatever, and introduced a sofa to render courtship more palatable and Turkish.

In 1776, a clergyman from one of the polite towns went into the country, and preached against the unchristian custom of young men and maidens lying together on a bed. He was no sooner out of the church than attacked by a shoal of good old women, with, 'Sir, do you think we and our daughters are naughty, because we allow bundling?'

'You lead yourselves into temptation by it.'

They all replied at once, 'Sir, have you been told thus, or has experience taught it you?'

The Levite began to lift up his eyes, and to consider of his situation, and bowing, said, 'I have been told so.'

The ladies, *una voce,* bawled out, 'Your informants, sir, we conclude, are those city ladies who prefer a sofa to a bed: we advise you to alter your sermon by substituting the word *sofa* for *bundling,* and on your return home preach it to them, for experience has told us that city folks send more children into the country without fathers or mothers than are born among us. Therefore you see a sofa is more dangerous than a bed.'

The poor priest, seemingly convinced of his blunder, exclaimed, '*Nec vitia nostra, nec remedia pati possumus,*'* hoping thereby to get rid of his guests, but an old matron pulled off her spectacles, and, looking the priest in the face like a Roman heroine, said, '*Noli putare me hoec auribus tuis dare.*'†

---

*We can endure neither our vices nor their remedies.
†Don't think I am saying this for your ears.

2   *Prophecies*

Democracy

It is certainly a great truth that man's original liberty, after it is resigned, ought to be cherished in all wise governments; or otherwise a man, in making himself a subject, alters himself from a freeman into a slave, which is repugnant to the law of nature. Also, the natural equality of men amongst men must be duly favored, in that government was never established by God or nature to give one man a prerogative to insult over another. Therefore, in a civil, as well as a natural, state of being, a just equality is to be indulged so far that every man is bound to honor every man, which is agreeable both with nature and religion.

The end of all good government is to cultivate humanity, and promote the happiness of all, and the good of every man in all his rights, his life, liberty, estate, honor &c., without injury or abuse to any.

ANTI-SLAVERY PAMPHLET, 1700: The Selling of Joseph

For as much as Liberty is in real value next unto Life, none ought to part with it themselves or deprive others of it, but upon the most mature consideration.

The numerousness of slaves at this day in the Province, and the uneasiness of them under their slavery, hath put many upon thinking whether the foundation of it be well and firmly laid, so as to sustain the vast weight that is built upon it. It is most certain that all men, as they are the sons of Adam, are co-heirs, and have equal right unto liberty and all other outward comforts of life. *God hath given the earth* (with all its commodities) *unto the sons of Adam.* PSALM 115, 16. *And hath made of one blood all nations of men, for to dwell on all the face of the earth.* ACTS 17, 26.

So that originally, and naturally, there is no such thing as slavery. Joseph was rightfully no more a slave to his brethren than they were to him, and they had no more authority, to *sell* him than they had to *slay* him. And if they had nothing to do to sell him, the Ishmaelites bargaining with them and paying down twenty pieces of silver could not make a title. There is no proportion between twenty pieces of silver and Liberty.

It is likewise most lamentable to think how in taking Negroes out of Africa and selling of them here, that which God has joined together men do boldly rend asunder: men from their country, husbands from their wives, parents from their children. How horrible is the uncleanness, mortality, if not murder, that the ships are guilty of that bring great crowds of these miserable men and women.

THE REVEREND JOHN WISE
A Vindication of the Government of New England Churches, Boston, 1717.

JUDGE SAMUEL SEWALL
The Selling of Joseph; a Memorial, Boston, 1700.

AMERICA, 1758

America is a subject which daily becomes more and more interesting. I shall therefore fill these pages with a word upon its past, present, and future state.

First, of its past state: Time has cast a shade upon this scene. Since the Creation innumerable accidents have happened here, the bare mention of which would create wonder and surprise, but they are all lost in oblivion. The ignorant natives for want of letters have forgot their stock, and know not whence they came, or how, or when they arrived here, or what has happened since.

Who can tell what wonderful changes have happened by the mighty operations of nature, such as deluges, volcanoes, earthquakes, &c.! Or whether great tracts of land were not absorbed into those vast lakes or inland seas which occupy so much space to the west of us.

Secondly, the present state of North America: That fertile country to the west of the Appalachian Mountains is of larger extent than all France, Germany, and Poland, and all well provided with rivers, a very wholesome air, a rich soil—in fine, the garden of the world! Time was when we might have been possessed of it. At this time two mighty kings contend for this inestimable prize. Their respective claims are to be measured by the length of their swords.

Our numbers will not avail till the colonies are united. If we do not join heart and hand in the common cause against our exulting foes, it may really happen as the Governor of Pennsylvania told his assembly: 'We shall have no privilege to dispute about, nor country to dispute in.'

Thirdly, of the future state of North America: The curious have observed that the progress of human literature, like the sun, is from the east to the west. Thus has it travelled through Asia and Europe and now is arrived at the eastern shore of America. So arts and sciences will change the face of nature in their tour from hence over the Appalachian Mountains to the Western Ocean; and as they march through the vast desert, the residence of wild beasts will be broken up, and their obscene howl cease forever. Instead of which, the stones and trees will dance together at the music of Orpheus—the rocks will disclose the hidden gems—and the inestimable treasures of gold and silver be broken up.

Huge mountains of iron are already discovered, and vast stores are reserved for future generations. This metal, more useful than gold and silver, will employ millions of hands, not only to form the martial sword and peaceful share alternately, but an infinity of utensils improved in the exercise of art and handicraft. Shall not then those vast quarries that teem with mechanic stone—those for structure—be piled into great cities, and those for sculpture into statues to perpetuate the honor of renowned heroes, even those who shall NOW save their country?

O ye unborn inhabitants of America! Should this page escape its destined conflagration at the year's end, and these alphabetical letters remain legible,—when your eyes behold the sun after he has rolled the seasons round for two or three centuries more, you will know that in Anno Domini 1758, we dreamed of your times.

NATHANIEL AMES
*An Astronomical Diary, or an Almanac
For the Year of Our Lord Christ 1758, Boston.*

3   Revolution

These are their bounds, which by God and Nature are fixed. Hitherto have they a right to come, and no further.

1. To govern by stated laws.
2. Those laws should have no other end ultimately but the good of the people.
3. Taxes are not to be laid on the people but by their consent in person or by deputation.
4. Their whole power is not transferable.

These are the first principles of law and justice, and the great barriers of a free state, and of the British constitution in particular. I ask, I want no more.

Now let it be shown how 'tis reconcilable with these fundamental maxims of the British constitution that all the northern colonies, who are without one representative in the House of Commons, should be taxed by the British parliament.

That the colonists, black and white, born here, are freeborn British subjects, and entitled to all the essential civil rights of such, is a truth not only manifest from the provincial charters, from the principles of the common law, and acts of parliament, but from the British constitution, which professed to secure the liberties of all the subjects to all generations.

JAMES OTIS
The Rights of the British Colonies Asserted and Proved,
Boston, 1764.

The year 1765 has been the most remarkable year of my life. That enormous engine, fabricated by the British parliament for battering down all the rights and liberties of America, I mean the Stamp Act, has raised and spread through the whole continent a spirit that will be recorded to our honor with all future generations. In every colony from Georgia to New Hampshire inclusively, the stamp distributers and inspectors have been compelled by the unconquerable rage of the people to resign their offices.

The people, even the lowest ranks, have become more attentive to their liberties, more inquisitive about them, and more determined to defend them, than they were ever before known or had occasion to be; innumerable have been the monuments of wit, humor, sense, learning, spirit, patriotism, and heroism erected in the several colonies and provinces in the course of this year. Our presses have groaned, our pulpits have thundered, our legislatures have resolved, our towns have voted; the crown officers have everywhere trembled, and all their little tools and creatures been afraid to speak and ashamed to be seen.

DEDICATION OF A TREE OF LIBERTY, PROVIDENCE, RHODE ISLAND, 1768

We do therefore, in the name and behalf of all true Sons of Liberty in America, or wheresoever they are dispersed throughout the world, dedicate and solemnly devote this tree, to be a Tree of Liberty.

May all our counsels and deliberations under its venerable branches be guided by wisdom, and directed to the support and maintenance of that liberty which our renowned forefathers sought out and found under trees and in the wilderness.

May it long flourish, and may the Sons of Liberty often repair thither to confirm and strengthen each other. When they look toward this sacred Elm, may they be penetrated with a sense of their duty to themselves, their country, and their posterity.

JOHN ADAMS
Diary. In *Works,* Boston, 1850, vol. II.
A SON OF LIBERTY

THE BOSTON MASSACRE

I, Sarah Wilme, of lawful age, testify that about ten days before the late massacre Christopher Rumbly of the 14th regiment was at our house and did talk very much against the Town, and said, if there should be any interruption, that the grenadiers company was to march up King Street; and that he would level his piece so as not to miss; and said that the blood would soon run in the streets of Boston.

I, Robert Polley, of lawful age, testify and declare that on Monday evening the 5th instant we met in the alley eight or nine soldiers, some of whom were armed with drawn swords and cutlasses, one had a tongs, another a shovel, with which they assaulted us, and gave us a good deal of abusive language. We then drove them back to the barracks with sticks only. We looked for stones or bricks, but could find none, the ground being covered with snow. Some of the lads dispersed, and myself with a few others were returning peaceably, when we met about nine or ten other soldiers armed with a naked cutlass in one hand and a stick or bludgeon in the other; one of them said, 'Where are the sons of bitches?' They struck at several persons in the street and went towards the head of the alley.

I, Thomas Marshall, being in my shop at the front of the house, I heard the cry of Murder at a distance, on which I opened the door, but saw no person in the street. But in half a minute, I saw several persons rushing out from the main guardhouse, crying out, 'Damn them, where are they?' They came down as far as the corner of Mr Phillips' house; I saw their swords and bayonets glitter in the moonlight, crying out as before, '—And by Jesus let them come!' at which time I was called into the house by one of my family, but returned in half a minute, and saw ten or twelve soldiers in a tumultuous manner in the middle of King Street, opposite Royal Exchange Lane, flourishing their arms and saying, 'Damn them, where are they?' and crying 'Fire!'; the bells then rung as if for fire.

I, John Coburn, being alarmed by the cry of fire and ringing of bells, ran out of my house with my bags and buckets; upon going to Mr Payne's door, he told me it was not a fire, it was a riot. I then sent my buckets home again, and went to Mr Amory's corner with Mr Payne, and Mr Walker the builder came along and said the soldiers were in the street, in Cornhill and Dock Square, with their drawn cutlasses, cutting and slashing everybody in their way, and the inhabitants wanted help, and said, 'Pray, gentlemen, run!'

I, Charles Hobby, saw a party of soldiers loading their muskets about the custom house door, after which they all shouldered. I heard some of the inhabitants cry out, 'Heave no snowballs!'; others cried. 'They dare not fire!' Captain Preston was then standing by the soldiers, when a snowball struck a grenadier, who immediately fired, Captain Preston standing close by him. The Captain then spoke distinctly, 'Fire, fire!' I was then within four feet of Captain Preston, and know him well. The soldiers fired as fast as they could, one after another. I saw the Mulatto fall, and Mr Samuel Gray went to look at him. One of the soldiers, at the distance of four or five yards, pointed his piece directly for the said Gray's head and fired. Mr Gray, after struggling, turned himself right round upon his heel, and fell dead.

I, Nathaniel Fosdick, rushed in; then seeing the first soldier that fired run at some persons and fall upon the ground, I halloed to take his gun from him. Then I received three pushes by their bayonets, two on my left arm, and one in my breast; that at my breast I struck off with a stick, and the gun went off immediately.

I, John Hickling, turning, saw Mr Palmes upon his knees and the soldiers pushing at him with their bayonets. During this the rest of the guns were fired, one after another, when I saw two more fall. I ran to one, and seeing the blood gush out of his head, though just expiring, I felt for the wound, and found a hole as big as my hand; this I have since learned was Mr Gray. I then went to Attucks and found him gasping, I pulled his head out of the gutter, and left him; I returned to the soldiers and asked them what they thought of themselves, to lay men wallowing in their blood in such a manner. They answered, 'God damn them, they should have stood out of our way.' The soldiers were then loading their muskets, and told me upon my peril not to come any nearer to them.

I, Benjamin Burdick, Junior, carried off the dead without regarding the soldiers. I then saw an officer pass before the soldiers, and hove up their arms, and said, 'Stop firing; do not fire any more;' upon which they shouldered. I then went up close to them, and, addressing myself to the whole, told them I came to see some faces that I might be able to swear to another day. Captain Preston, who was the officer, turned round and answered (in a melancholy tone), 'Perhaps you may.' After taking a view of each man's face I left them.

A Short Narrative of the Horrid Massacre in Boston, perpetrated in the evening of the fifth day of March, 1770; printed by order of the Town of Boston, March, 1770. Withheld by Boston Town Meeting from publication until after the trials of the British soldiers, lest it prejudice those who should serve as jurors.

To Thomas Hutchinson, Royal Governor of the Massachusetts Colony

Letter—by John Adams?—written in the name of the first man killed in the Revolution, the Negro Chrispus Attucks.

Sir:—You will hear from us with astonishment. You ought to hear from us with horror. You are chargeable before God and man with our blood. The soldiers were but passive instruments, mere machines; neither moral nor voluntary in our destruction, more than the leaden pellets with which we were wounded. You was [sic] a free agent. You acted coolly, deliberately, with all the premeditated malice, not against us in particular, but against the people in general, which in the sight of the law is an ingredient in the compostion of murder. You will hear further from us hereafter.

CHRISPUS ATTUCKS
From John Adams, *Works,* Boston, 1850, vol. II.

Revolution

When I went home to my family in May, 1770, from the town meeting in Boston, which was the first I had ever attended, and where I had been chosen in my absence, without any solicitation, one of their representatives, I said to my wife, 'I have accepted a seat in the House of Representatives, and thereby have consented to my own ruin, to your ruin, and the ruin of our children. I give you this warning that you may prepare your mind for your fate.' She burst into tears, but instantly cried out in a transport of magnanimity, 'Well, I am willing in this cause to run all risks with you, and be ruined with you, if you are ruined.' These were times, my friend, in Boston, which tried women's souls as well as men's.

If the liberties of America are ever completely ruined, of which, in my opinion, there is now the utmost danger, it will in all probability be the consequence of a mistaken notion of prudence, which leads men to acquiesce in measures of the most destructive tendency for the sake of present ease.

When designs are formed to raze the very foundation of a free government, those few who are to erect their grandeur and fortune upon the general ruin will employ every art to soothe the devoted people into a state of indolence, inattention, and security, which is forever the forerunner of slavery. They are alarmed at nothing so much as attempts to awaken the people to jealousy and watchfulness; and it has been an old game, played over and over again, to hold up the men who would rouse their fellow citizens to a sense of their real danger, and spirit them to the most zealous activity in the use of all proper means for the preservation of the public liberty, as 'pretended patriots,' 'intemperate politicians,' rash hot-headed men, incendiaries, wretched desperadoes, who, as was once said of the best of men, would turn the world upside down, or have done it already.

JOHN ADAMS
Letter to Benjamin Rush, April 12, 1809.

SAMUEL ADAMS
Boston Gazette, December 9, 1771.

TEA PARTY

Boston, 17 December, 1773

The Committee of Correspondence of Boston to Other Committees of Correspondence:

Gentlemen:
Yesterday we had a greater meeting of the Body than ever, the country coming in from twenty miles around, and every step was taken that was practicable for returning the teas. The moment it was known out of doors that Mr Rotch could not obtain a pass for his ship by the Castle, a number of people huzza'd in the street, and in a very little time every ounce of the teas on board of the Captains Hall, Bruce, and Coffin, was immersed in the Bay, without the least injury to private property. The Spirit of the People on this occasion surprised all parties who viewed the same.

*In the name of the Committee
Samuel Adams*

CLOSING OF BOSTON PORT

January 25, 1774

The destruction of the tea is the pretence for the unprecedented severity shown to the Town of Boston, but the real cause is the opposition to tyranny for which the people of that town have always made themselves remarkable, and for which I think this country is much obliged to them. They are suffering the vengeance of Administration in the common cause of America.

July 25, 1774

Four regiments are encamped upon our Common, while the Harbor is blocked up by ships of war. Nothing is suffered to be waterborne in the Harbor excepting the wood and provisions brought in to keep us from actually perishing. By such oppressions the British Administration hope to suppress the Spirit of Liberty in this place, but, being encouraged by the generous supplies that are daily sent to us, the inhabitants are determined to hold out and appeal to the justice of the colonies and of the world, trusting in God that these things shall be overruled for the establishment of liberty, virtue, and happiness in America.

SAMUEL ADAMS
Writings, New York and London, 1906, vol. III.

Paul Revere: His Own Story

In the year 1773 I was employed by the Selectmen of the Town of Boston to carry the account of the Destruction of the Tea to New York, and afterward, 1774, to carry their despatches to New York and Philadelphia for calling a Congress.

In the fall of 1774 and winter 1775, I was one of upwards of thirty, chiefly mechanics, who formed ourselves into a committee for the purpose of watching the movement of the Tories. We held our meeting at the Green Dragon Tavern. We were so careful that our meetings should be kept secret that every time we met, every person swore upon the Bible that they would not discover any of our transactions but to Messrs Hancock, Adams, Doctors Warren, Church, and one or two more.

About November, when things began to grow serious, a gentleman who had connections with the Tory party but was a Whig at heart, acquainted me that our meetings were discovered, and mentioned the identical words that were spoken among us the night before. We did not then distrust Doctor Church, but supposed it must be someone among us. We removed to another place which we thought was more secure; but here we found that all our transactions were communicated to Governor Gage.

In the winter, towards the spring, we frequently took turns, two and two, to watch the soldiers by patrolling the streets all night. The Saturday night preceding the 19th of April, the boats belonging to the transports were all launched and carried under the sterns of the men-of-war; the Grenadiers and light infantry were all taken off duty. On Tuesday evening, the 18th, it was discovered that a number of soldiers were marching towards the bottom of the Common.

About 10 o'clock, Dr. Warren sent in great haste for me, and begged that I would immediately set off for Lexington, where Messrs Hancock and Adams were, and acquaint them of the movement, and that it was thought they were the objects. When I got to Dr Warren's house, I found he had sent an express by land to Lexington—a Mr William Daws. The Sunday before, I had been to Charlestown; there I agreed with some gentlemen that if the British went out by water, we would shew two lanthorns in the North Church steeple, and, if by land, one, as a signal. I left Dr Warren's, called upon a friend, and desired him to make the signals.

I then went home, took my boots and surtout, and went to the north part of the town, where I kept a boat. Two friends rowed me across Charles River, a little to the eastward where the *Somerset*, man-of-war, lay. It was then young flood, the ship was winding, and the moon was rising. They landed me on the Charlestown side. When I got to the town, they said they had seen our signals. I told them what was acting.

I set off upon a very good horse. It was then 11 o'clock and very pleasant. After I had passed Charlestown neck, I saw two men on horseback under a tree. When I got near them, I discovered they were British officers. One tried to git [sic] ahead of me and the other to take me. I turned my horse very quick, and galloped toward Charlestown neck. The one who chased me to cut me off got into a clay pond.

In Medford I awaked the captain of the Minute Men, and after that I alarmed almost every house till I got to Lexington. I found Messrs Hancock and Adams at the Rev. Mr Clark's. I told them my errand. After I had been there about half an hour, Mr Daws came. We refreshed ourselves, and set out for Concord, to secure the stores &c. there. We were overtaken by a young Dr Prescott, whom we found to be a high Son of Liberty.

Revolution

We had got nearly half way, Mr Daws and the Doctor stopped to alarm the people of a house, I was about one hundred rod ahead, when I saw two men. I called for the Doctor and Daws to come up. In an instant I was surrounded by four; they had placed themselves in a straight road that inclined each way; they had taken down a pair of bars on the north side of the road and two of them were under a tree in the pasture. We tried to git past them, but being armed with pistols and swords, they forced us into the pasture. The Doctor jumped his horse over a low stone wall, and got to Concord. I observed a wood at a small distance and made for that. Out started six officers on horseback and ordered me to dismount. One of them, who appeared to have the command, examined me, where I came from and what my name was? I told him. He asked me if I was an express. I answered in the affirmative. He demanded what time I left Boston? I told him, and added that their troops had catched aground in passing the river, and that there would be five hundred Americans there in a short time, for I had alarmed the country all the way up.

He then ordered them to advance and lead me in front; if I attempted to run, or anybody insulted them, to blow my brains out. We rode till we got near Lexington Meeting House, when the militia fired a volley of guns, which appeared to alarm them very much. The Sargent mounted my horse, when they all rode towards Lexington Meeting House. I went across the Burying Ground and some pastures, and came to the Rev. Mr Clark's house, where I found Messrs Hancock and Adams. I told them of my treatment and they concluded to go from that house.

To git a trunk of papers belonging to Mr Hancock, we went up chamber, and while gitting the trunk, we saw the British very near, upon a full march. We hurried; on our way we passed through the militia. There were about 50.

When we had got about 100 yards from the Meeting House, the British troops appeared on both sides. In their front was an officer on horseback. They made a short halt when I saw, and heard, a gun fired, which appeared to be a pistol. Then I could distinguish two guns, and then a continual roar of musketry; when we made off with the trunk.

A Son of Liberty in the Year 1775
Paul Revere

PAUL REVERE
Letter to Reverend Jeremy Belknap.

TICONDEROGA

Ever since I arrived at the state of manhood, and acquainted myself with the general history of mankind, I have felt a sincere passion for liberty. The history of nations doomed to perpetual slavery in consequence of yielding up to tyrants their natural born liberties, I read with a sort of philosophical horror; so that the first systemical and bloody attempt, at Lexington, to enslave America, thoroughly electrified my mind. And, while I was wishing for an opportunity to signalize myself, directions were privately sent me to raise the Green Mountain Boys and, if possible, with them surprise and take the fortress of Ticonderoga.

I arrived at the lake opposite to Ticonderoga on the evening of the ninth day of May, 1775, with two hundred and thirty valiant Green Mountain Boys. It was with the utmost difficulty that I procured boats to cross the lake. However, I landed eighty-three men near the garrison and sent the boats back for the rear guard, but the day began to dawn and I found myself under the necessity to attack before the rear guard could cross the lake. As it was viewed hazardous, I harangued the officers and soldiers, in the manner following:

'Friends and fellow soldiers, you have for a number of years past been a scourge and terror to arbitrary power. Your valor has been famed abroad, and acknowledged, as appears by the orders to me from the General Assembly of Connecticut to surprise and take the garrison now before us. I propose to advance before you and, in person, conduct you through the wicket-gate. We must this morning either quit our pretensions to valor or possess ourselves of this fortress in a few minutes; and, inasmuch as it is a desperate attempt, which none but the bravest dare undertake, I do not urge it on any contrary to his will. You that will undertake voluntarily, poise your firelocks.'

Each poised his firelock. I ordered them to face to the right and marched them immediately to the wicket-gate aforesaid, where I found a sentry posted, who instantly snapped his fusee at me. I ran toward him and he retreated through the covered way into the parade within the garrison, gave a halloo, and ran under a bombproof. My party, who followed me into the fort, I formed to face the two barracks. The garrison being asleep, except the sentries, we gave three huzzas which greatly surprised them. One of the sentries made a pass at one of my officers with a charged bayonet and slightly wounded him. My first thought was to kill him with my sword, but in an instant altered the design and fury of the blow to a slight cut on the side of the head. He dropped his gun and asked quarter. I demanded of him the place where the commanding officer kept; he showed me a pair of stairs to which I immediately repaired and ordered the commander, Capt. de la Place, to come forth instantly. The Captain came to the door with his breeches in his hand. I ordered him to deliver me the fort instantly. He asked me by what authority I demanded it. I answered him. *'In the name of the great Jehovah and the Continental Congress.'*

He began to speak again, but I interrupted him, and with my drawn sword over his head, again demanded an immediate surrender. He then complied, and ordered his men to be forthwith paraded without arms. In the mean time, some of my officers had given orders, sundry of the barrack doors were beat down, and about one-third of the garrison imprisoned.

This surprise was carried into execution in the grey of the morning of the tenth day of May, 1775. The sun seemed to rise that morning with a superior lustre, and Ticonderoga smiled to its conquerors, who tossed the flowing bowl and wished success to Congress and the liberty and freedom of America.

ETHAN ALLEN
A Narrative of Colonel Ethan Allen's Captivity, Boston, 1779.

TRIAL OF A TORY IN VERMONT

One David Redding had been accused of supplying the enemy on the lakes with provisions and several other acts unfriendly to the country. He was at first tried by a jury of *six* persons, convicted, and sentenced to be hung on the sixth day of June, 1778. In the meantime, John Burnam, an attorney at law, who had recently arrived from Connecticut with Blackstone's Commentaries in his saddle-bags, appeared before the council of safety and showed them that Redding's conviction had been irregular, inasmuch as no man could be legally convicted of a capital crime but by twelve jurymen. The council, perceiving their error, granted a new trial.

No execution had ever taken place in Vermont. The intelligence that a new trial had been granted was received at the moment when the excited throng were collecting to witness the execution. With such a multitude and on such an occasion it was useless to talk of law. They had pronounced the culprit guilty and were preparing to seize the prisoner and unceremoniously hang him.

Upon this, Ethan Allen pressed through the crowd, mounted a stump, and, waving his hat, exclaimed in thundering tones, 'Attention, the whole!'

Silence was at one restored. He then proceeded to announce the reasons which had produced the reprieve, advised the multitude to depart peaceably to their habitations, and return on the day fixed for the execution, adding with a tremendous oath: 'You shall see somebody hung, at all events. If Redding is not then hung, I will be hung myself!'

The crowd quickly dispersed, and, after having been a second time convicted, Redding was finally executed.

To her husband, John Adams   31 July 1777

A new set of mobility has lately taken the lead in Boston. There is a great scarcity of sugar and coffee, articles which the female part of the State is very loathe to give up. There has been much rout and noise in the town for several weeks. Some stores had been opened by a number of people, and the coffee and sugar carried into the market and dealt out by pounds. It was rumored that an eminent, wealthy, stingy merchant (who is a bachelor) had a hogshead of coffee in his store which he refused to sell to the committee under six shillings a pound.

A number of females, some say a hundred, some say more, assembled with a cart and trucks, marched down to the warehouse, and demanded the keys, which he refused to deliver. One of them seized him by his neck and tossed him into the cart. Upon his finding no quarter, he delivered the keys, when they tipped up the cart and discharged him; then opened the warehouse, hoisted out the coffee themselves, put it in the trucks, and drove off. It was reported that he had personal chastisement among them; but this I believe was not true. A large concourse of men stood amazed, silent spectators of the whole transaction.

31 March 1776

I long to hear that you have declared an independency. And, by the way, in the new code of laws which I suppose it will be necessary for you to make, I desire you would remember the ladies and be more generous to them than your ancestors. Do not put such unlimited power into the hands of the husbands. Remember, all men would be tyrants if they could. If particular care and attention is not paid to the ladies, we are determined to foment a rebellion, and will not hold ourselves bound by any laws in which we have no voice or representation.

HENRY W. DE PUY
Ethan Allen and the Green Mountain Heroes of '76, Boston, 1853.

ABIGAIL ADAMS
Letters.

DRAFTING THE DECLARATION OF INDEPENDENCE

You inquire why so young a man as Mr Jefferson was placed at the head of the committee for preparing a Declaration of Independence? I answer: It was the advice, to place Virginia at the head of everything. There were three committees appointed at the same time. One for the Declaration of Independence, another for preparing articles of Confederation, and another for preparing a treaty to be proposed to France.

Mr Jefferson came into Congress in June, 1775, and brought with him a reputation for literature, science, and a happy talent of composition. Writings of his were handed about, remarkable for the peculiar felicity of expression. Though a silent member in Congress, he was so prompt, frank, explicit, and decisive upon committees and in conversation—not even Samuel Adams was more so—that he soon seized upon my heart. And upon this occasion I gave him my vote, and did all in my power to procure the votes of others. I think he had one more vote than any other, and that placed him at the head of the committee. I had the next highest number and that placed me second. The committee met, discussed the subject, and then appointed Mr Jefferson and me to make the draft.

Jefferson proposed to me to make the draft. I said. 'I will not.' 'You should do it.' 'Oh! no.' 'Why will you not?' 'Reasons enough.' 'What can be your reasons?' 'Reason first—You are a Virginian, and a Virginian ought to appear at the head of this business. Reason second—I am obnoxious, suspected, and unpopular. You are very much otherwise. Reason third—You can write ten times better than I can.' 'Well,' said Jefferson, 'if you are decided, I will do as well as I can.' 'Very well. When you have drawn it up, we will have a meeting.'

A meeting we accordingly had, and conned the paper over. I was delighted with its high tone and the flights of oratory with which it abounded, especially that concerning Negro slavery, which, though I knew his Southern brethren would never suffer to pass in Congress, I certainly never would oppose. There were other expressions which I would not have inserted, if I had drawn it up, particularly that which called the King tyrant. I never believed George to be a tyrant in disposition and nature; I always believed him to be deceived by his courtiers on both sides of the Atlantic, and in his official capacity only, cruel. I thought the expression too passionate, and too much like scolding, for so grave and solemn a document, but as Franklin and Sherman were to inspect it afterwards, I consented to report it and do not now remember that I made or suggested a single alteration.

We reported it to the committee of five, and I do not remember that Franklin or Sherman criticized anything. We were all in haste. Congress was impatient, and the instrument was reported, as I believe, in Jefferson's handwriting, as he first drew it. Congress cut off about a quarter of it, as I expected they would: they obliterated some of the best of it, and left all that was unexceptional, if anything in it was. I have long wondered that the original draft has not been published. I suppose the reason is the violent philippic against Negro slavery.

As you justly observe, there is not an idea in it but what had been hackneyed in Congress for two years before. The substance of it is contained in the declaration of rights, and the violation of those rights, in the Journals of Congress, in 1774. Indeed, the essence of it is contained in a pamphlet, voted and printed by the town of Boston, before the first Congress met, composed by James Otis, as I suppose, in one of his lucid intervals, and pruned and polished by Samuel Adams.

Your friend and humble servant,
John Adams

JOHN ADAMS
Letter to Timothy Pickering, August 6, 1822.

PART THREE

I Hill and Town

JOURNEY TO CONNECTICUT

Autumn of 1789

The road is hilly and rocky until we reach the upper meeting house, where it suddenly alters to a level without any stones. After passing a burial ground, it ascends the Western Mountains, a ridge that intersects the state and terminates in Connecticut. This pass is about five and one-half miles over, and we were an hour and a half in crossing it. In some places it is a solid mass of rock. One can scarcely believe this has been the main road to Springfield from time immemorial.

Powers's in Brimfield is not a stage inn. It was late and we had no other choice. Our repast was various: cold meat, corn, baked apples, wild honey, eggs, cheese, etc. The room in which we dined recalled Dr Goldsmith's description. There was the 'bed by night, the chest of drawers by day'; and among its decorations were an 'Elegy on a Late Hurricane' and 'Handsome Harry, or the Deceitful Young Man.' The good dame of the house talked much and loud. Some new cheeses appeared to be inlaid with sprigs and flowers. I asked the landlady how it was done. She said. 'The little witch of a girl brought the leaves from the garden and when the cheese was soft pressed them in.' The effect was pleasing and to me new; the good woman, it seems, thought otherwise.

Sept. 24.

The frontier town of Connecticut. Stone walls again appear. A morning prospect from a hill in Westminister Society: the sun was rising, while the vapors of the night rested in the valleys like a vast lake interspersed with islands. The risen day soon dissipated these vapors, when were successively exhibited forests, spires, and cultivation.

SAMUEL DAVIS
Massachusetts Historical Society, *Proceedings*, 1869-70.

JOURNEY TO VERMONT

Spring of 1789

Friday entered the State of Vermont—a bad appearance at the entrance—miserable set of inhabitants—no religion—Monday 3 of May journeyed to Manchester, half shire town hemmed in by lofty mountains—loose town—

I was greatly worried and fatigued with riding—poor living—nothing but brook water to drink—and no comfortable victuals—my nature almost exhausted.

Came to Governor Chittenden's. A low poor house, a plain family and low, vulgar man, clownish, excessively parsimonious—made me welcome—hard fare, a very great farm—1000 acres, hundred acres of wheat on the Onion river—200 acres of extraordinary interval land. A shrewd cunning man—skilled in human nature and in agriculture —understands extremely well the mysteries of Vermont.

About 300 towns in the State of Vermont—about 40 of the towns upon the Green Mountains—very cold—snow upon the top of them until June—about as many as 40 families in a town, upon an average.

No cheese anywhere—no beef—no butter—I pine for home—for my own table. Words cannot describe the hardships I undergo—

Got lost in the woods already—heard the horrible howling of the wolves. Far absent—in the wilderness—among all strangers—all alone—among log-huts—people nasty—poor—low-lived—indelicate—and miserable cooks.

All sadly parsimonious—many profane—yet cheerful and much more contented than in Hartford—and the women more contented than the men—turned tawny by the smoke of the log-huts—dress coarse, and mean, and nasty, and ragged. Some very clever women and men—serious and sensible. Scarcely any sensible preaching—will settle Ministers in most of the towns—and in a few years be a good Country, pleasant and well to live in—

When I go from hut to hut, from town to town, in the wilderness, the people nothing to eat—to drink—or wear—all work, and yet the women quiet—serene—peaceable —contented, loving their husbands—their homes—wanting never to return—nor any dressy clothes; I think how strange!—I ask myself are these women of the same species with our fine Ladies? Tough are they, brawny their limbs —their young girls unpolished—and will bear work as well as mules. Woods make people love one another and kind and obliging and good natured. They set much more store by one another than in the old settlement. Leave their doors unbarred. Sleep quietly amid—dirt and rags.

THE REVEREND NATHAN PERKINS

WINTER DANCE

Portland, Maine, 1 March, 1802

Such a frolic! Such a chain of adventures I never before met with. Thursday it snowed violently—indeed for two days before it had been storming so much that the snowdrifts were very large; however, as it was the last assembly, I could not resist the temptation of going, as I knew all the world would be there.

About seven I went downstairs and found young Charles Coffin, the minister, in the parlor. After the usual inquiries were over, he stared awhile at my feathers and flowers, asked if I was going out. I told him I was going to the assembly. 'Think, Miss Southgate,' said he, after a long pause, 'do you think you would go out to *meeting* in such a storm as this?' Then assuming a tone of reproof, he entreated me to examine well my feelings on such an occasion. I heard in silence, unwilling to begin an argument that I was unable to support. The stopping of the carriage roused me; I immediately slipped on my socks and coat and met Horatio and Mr Motley in the entry. The snow was deep, but Mr Motley took me up in his arms and sat me in the carriage without difficulty.

I found a full assembly, many married ladies, and everyone disposed to end the winter in good spirits. At one we left dancing and went to the card-room to wait for a coach. It stormed dreadfully; the hacks were all employed as soon as they returned, and we could not get one till three o'clock, for about two they left the house, determined not to return again for the night. It was the most violent storm I ever knew, there were now twenty in waiting, the gentlemen scolding and fretting, the ladies murmuring and complaining.

One hack returned; all flocked to the stairs to engage a seat. So many crowded down that 'twas impossible to get past; luckily I was one of the first. Sister had so much company that I was obliged to go home with Sally Weeks and give my chamber to Parson Coffin.

None but ladies were permitted to get into the carriage; it presently was stowed in [so] full that the horses could not move. The door was burst open, for such a clamor as the closing of it occasioned I never before heard; the universal cry was—'A gentleman in the coach,' 'Let him come out.' We all protested there was none, as it was too dark to distinguish—but the little man soon raised his voice and bid the coachman proceed. A dozen voices gave contrary orders—'twas a proper riot. A gentleman at the door jumped into the carriage, caught hold of him, and would have dragged him out if we had not all entreated them to desist. He squeezed again into his seat, inwardly exulting to think he should get safe home from such rough creatures as the men, should pass for a lady, be secure under their protections for none would insult him before them—mean creature!

The carriage at length started, full of ladies and not one gentleman to protect us—except our ladyman who had crept to us for shelter. Luckily, two gentlemen had followed by the side of the carriage, and when it stopped took out the ladies as they got to their houses. Our sweet little trembling, delicate, unprotected fellow sat immovable while the two gentlemen, that were obliged to walk through all the snow and storm, carried all the ladies from the coach.

The storm continued until Monday, and I was obliged to stay—but Monday I insisted, if there was any possibility of getting to sister's, to set out. The horse and sleigh were soon at the door, and again I sallied forth to brave the tempestuous weather (for it still snowed). At length we arrived at sister Boyd's door, and the drift before it was the greatest we had met with. The horse was so exhausted that he sunk down. 'Twas some distance from the gate and no path; the gentleman took me up in his arms and carried me until my weight pressed him so far into the snow that he had no power to move his feet. I rolled out of his arms, and wallowed till I reached the gate; then rising to shake off the snow, I turned and beheld my beau fixed and immovable; he could not get his feet out to take another step. By this time all the family had gathered to the window—indeed, they saw the whole frolic; but 'twas not yet ended, for unluckily, in pulling off Miss Weeks' bonnet to send to the sleigh to be carried back, I pulled off my wig and left my head bare. I was perfectly convulsed with laughter; think what a ludicrous figure I must have been—still standing at the gate—my bonnet halfway to the sleigh and my wig in my hand! However, I hurried it on—for they were all laughing at the window—and made the best of my way into the house.

ELIZA SOUTHGATE BOWNE
A Girl's Life Eighty Years Ago, New York, 1887.

MILL-GIRL

I went to my first day's work in the mill with a light heart. The novelty of it made it seem easy, and it really was not hard, just to change the bobbins on the spinning-frames every three quarters of an hour or so, with half a dozen other little girls who were doing the same thing. When I came back at night, the family began to pity me for my long, tiresome day's work, but I laughed and said,—

'Why, it is nothing but fun. It is just like play.'

And for a little while it was only a new amusement. And there was a great deal of play mixed with it. We were not occupied more than half the time. The intervals were spent frolicking around among the spinning-frames, teasing and talking to the older girls, or entertaining ourselves with games and stories in a corner, or exploring, with the overseer's permission, the mysteries of the carding-room, the dressing-room, and the weaving-room.

I never cared much for machinery. The buzzing and hissing and whizzing of pulleys and rollers and spindles and flyers around me often grew tiresome. But in a room below us we were sometimes allowed to peer in through a sort of blind door at the great water-wheel that carried the works of the whole mill. It was so huge that we could only watch a few of its spokes at a time, and part of its dripping rim, moving with a slow, measured strength through the darkness that shut it in. It impressed me with something of the awe which comes to us in thinking of the great Power which keeps the mechanism of the universe in motion.

I had learned to do a spinner's work, and I obtained permission to tend some frames that stood directly in front of the river-windows. I kept myself occupied with the river, my work, and my thoughts. And the river and my thoughts flowed on together. Like a loitering pilgrim, it sparkled up to me and bore away my little frets and fatigues on its bosom. When the 'work went well,' I sat in the window-seat, and let my fancies fly—downward to the sea, or upward to the hills that hid the mountain-cradle of the Merrimack.

The printed regulations forbade us to bring books into the mill, so I made my window-seat into a small library of poetry, pasting its sides all over with newspaper clippings. Some of the girls could not believe that the Bible was meant to be counted among forbidden books. We all thought that the Scriptures had a right to go wherever we went, and that if we needed them anywhere, it was at our work. I evaded the law by carrying some leaves from a torn Testament in my pocket.

The overseer, caring more for law than gospel, confiscated all he found. He had his desk full of Bibles. It sounded oddly to hear him say to the most religious girl in the room, when he took hers away, 'I did think you had more conscience than to bring that book here.'

The last window in the row behind me was filled with flourishing house-plants—fragrant-leaved geraniums, the overseer's pets. They gave that corner a bowery look; the perfume and freshness tempted me there often. Standing before that window, I could look across the room and see girls moving backwards and forwards among the spinning-frames, sometimes stooping, sometimes reaching up their arms, as their work required, with easy and not ungraceful movements. The girls were bright-looking and neat, and everything was kept clean and shining.

LUCY LARCOM
A New England Girlhood, Boston, 1899.

HUCKLER'S ROW

I come along towards the upper part of the town where there were stores and shops of all sorts and sizes. And I met a feller, and says I, what place is this? Why this, says he, is Huckler's Row.

Well then, thinks I to myself, I have a pesky good mind to go in and have a try with one of these chaps, and see if they can twist my eye-teeth out. If they can get the best end of a bargain out of me, they can do what there aint a man in Downingville can do, and I should jest like to know what sort of stuff these ere Portland chaps are made of.

So in I goes into the best-looking store among 'em. And I see some biscuit lying on the shelf, and says I, Mister, how much do you ax apiece for them are biscuit? A cent apiece, says he. Well, says I, I shant give you that, but if you've a mind to, I'll give you two cents for three of 'em, for I begin to feel a little as though I should like to take a bite. Well, says he, I wouldn't sell 'em to anybody else so, but seeing it's you, I don't care if you take 'em. I knew he lied, for he never see me before in his life.

Well, he handed down the biscuits and I took 'em, and walked round the store a while to see what else he had to sell. At last, says I, Mister, have you got any good new cider? Says he, yes, as good as ever you see. Well, says I, what do you ax a glass for it? Two cents, says he. Well, says I, seems to me I feel more dry than I do hungry now. Aint you a mind to take these ere biscuit again and give me a glass of cider? And says he, I dont care if I do; so he took and laid 'em on the shelf again, and poured out a glass of cider. I took the cider and drinkt it down, and to tell the truth it was capital good cider.

Then, says I, I guess it's time for me to be a going, and I stept along towards the door. But, says he, stop, Mister. I believe you haven't paid me for the cider. Not paid you for the cider, says I, what do you mean by that? Didn't the biscuit that I give you jest come to the cider? Oh, ah, right, says he. So I started to go again; and says he, but stop, Mister, you didn't pay me for the biscuit. What, says I, do you mean to impose on me? Do you think I am going to pay you for the biscuit and let you keep 'em tu? Aint they there now on your shelf, what more do you want? I guess, sir, you don't whittle me that way.

So I turned about and marched off, and left the fellow staring and thinking and scratching his head, as though he was struck with a dunderment. Howsomever, I didn't want to cheat him, only jest to show 'em it want so easy a matter to pull my eye-teeth out, so I called in next day, and paid him his two cents.

SEBA SMITH
Life and Writings of Major Jack Downing of Downingville, State of Maine, Boston, 1833.

Diary of the Learned Blacksmith

Worcester, Mass. Saturday, Aug. 21, 1841

Very warm, faint weather; feel sweaty and worn out. Studied Armenian. Have forged 11 hours.

Wed. April 26, 1843

I finished my Danish document to my great satisfaction and relief. I have laboured upon it for a fortnight constantly, and if I get nothing for my labour but the ability to translate Danish and German manuscripts I shall deem myself rewarded. Forged in the afternoon.

Monday, May 1st

The storm increased almost to a tempest this morning. Read Arabic and translated from the German until noon; worked upon my hoes till tea time.

Tuesday (May) 23

Read Arabic and wrote a page on my Peace lecture. This indeed is snail-like progress, but if unremitting, it will come to something in the end. In the afternoon I forged 5 hoes in 3 hours.

(Boston) Wednesday (June) 28

In the evening I delivered my new Peace lecture with all the effect I ever anticipated. It chained the audience for 1½ hours. Several of the first men of Boston were present and testified to their gratification in a very expressive manner.

Monday (July) 17

Read Gaelic and wrote a little on my lecture upon the *dignity* of manual labour.

(Worcester) Wednesday, Jan. 1st, 1845

I have entered upon another year. I find my mind is setting with all its sympathies towards the subject of Peace. I am persuaded that it is reserved to crown the destiny of America, that she shall be the great peace maker in the brotherhood of nations. And I think that I cannot better employ the talents and time that God may give me than to devote a year or two to this cause. I have therefore conceived a design of making a tour through the Western Country this winter, with the view of presenting the principles and objects of Peace.

ELIHU BURRITT
Diary.

EZRA RIPLEY, D.D., 1751-1841

I am sure all who remember both will associate his form with whatever was grave and droll in the old, cold, unpainted, uncarpeted, squarepewed meeting-house, with its four iron-gray deacons in their little box under the pulpit,—with Watts' hymns, with long prayers, rich with the diction of ages; and not less with the report like musketry from the movable seats.

One August afternoon, when I was in his hayfield helping him with his man to rake up his hay, I well remember his pleading, almost reproachful looks at the sky, when the thundergust was coming up to spoil his hay. He raked very fast, then looked at the cloud, and said, 'We are in the Lord's hand; mind your rake, George! We are in the Lord's hand'; and seemed to say, 'You know me, this field is mine,—Dr Ripley's—thine own servant!'

He used to tell the story of one of his old friends, the minister of Sudbury, who, being at the Thursday lecture in Boston, heard the officiating clergyman praying for rain. As soon as the service was over, he went up to the petitioner, and said, 'You Boston ministers, as soon as a tulip wilts under your windows, go to church and pray for rain, until all Concord and Sudbury are under water.'

His partiality for ladies was always strong, and was by no means abated by time. He claimed privilege of years, was much addicted to kissing; spared neither maid, wife, nor widow, and, as a lady thus favored, remarked to me, 'seemed as if he was going to make a meal of you.'

We remember the remark made by the old farmer who used to travel hither from Maine, that no horse from the Eastern country would go by his door. Travellers from the West and North and South bear the like testimony. His brow was serene and open to his visitor, for he loved men, and he had no studies, no occupations, which company could interrupt. His friends were his study, and to see them loosened his talents and his tongue.

In his house* dwelt order and prudence and plenty. There was no waste and no stint. He was open-handed and just and generous. Ingratitude and meanness in his beneficiaries did not wear out his compassion; he bore the insult, and the next day his basket for the beggar, his horse and chaise for the cripple, were at their door. Though he knew the value of a dollar as well as another man, yet he loved to buy dearer and sell cheaper than others.

In debate, in the vestry or the Lyceum, the structure of his sentences was admirable; so neat, so natural, so terse, his words fell like stones; and often, though quite unconscious of it, his speech was a satire on the loose, voluminous, draggle-tail periods of other speakers. He sat down when he had done.

An eminent skill he had in saying difficult and unspeakable things; in delivering to a man or a woman that which all their friends had abstained from saying, in uncovering the bandage from a sore place, and applying the surgeon's knife with a truly surgical spirit. Was a man a sot, or a spendthrift, or too long time a bachelor, or suspected of some hidden crime, or had he quarrelled with his wife, or collared his father, or was there any cloud or suspicious circumstance in his behavior, the good pastor knew his way straight to that point, believing himself entitled to a full explanation, and whatever relief to the conscience of both parties plain speech could effect was sure to be procured. In all such passages he justified himself to the conscience, and commonly to the love, of the persons concerned. He knew everybody's grandfather and seemed to address each person rather as the representative of his house and name, than as an individual.

And now, in his old age, when all the antique Hebraism and its customs are passing away, it is fit that he too should depart,—most fit that in the fall of laws a loyal man should die.

* The Old Manse, Concord.

RALPH WALDO EMERSON
From *Lectures and Biographical Sketches,* 1883. Quoted from an address to the Social Circle, Concord, Massachusetts, by Ezra Ripley's step-grandson.

MARY MOODY EMERSON, 1775-1869

When I read Dante, the other day, and his paraphrases to signify with more adequateness Christ or Jehovah, whom do you think I was reminded of? Whom but Mary Emerson and her eloquent theology? 'My opinion,' she writes [of Byron, is] 'that the fiery depths of Calvinism, its high and mysterious elections to eternal bliss, beyond angels, and all its attendant wonders, would have been alone fitted to fix his imagination.' She calls herself 'the puny pilgrim, whose sole talent is sympathy.'

When she met a young person who interested her, she made herself acquainted and intimate with him or her at once, by sympathy, by flattery, by raillery, by anecdotes, by wit, by rebuke, and stormed the castle. Scorn trifles, lift your aims; do what you are afraid to do; sublimity of character must come from sublimity of motive: these were the lessons which were urged with vivacity, in ever new language. But if her companion were dull, her impatience knew no bounds. If her companion were a little ambitious and asked her opinion on books or matters on which she did not wish rude hands laid, she did not hesitate to stop the intruder with 'How's your cat, Mrs Tenner?'

She had the misfortune of spinning with a greater velocity than any of the other tops. She would tear into the chaise or out of it, into the house or out of it, into the conversation, into the thought, into the character of the stranger—disdaining all the graduation by which her fellows time their steps: and though she might do very happily on a planet where others moved with the like velocity, she was offended here by the phlegm of all her fellow creatures, and disgusted them with her impatience. She could keep step with no human being. Her nephew [C.C.E.] wrote of her: 'By society with her, one's mind is electrified and purged. She is no statute-book of practical commandments, nor orderly digest of any system of philosophy, divine or human, but a Bible.'

She writes: 'August 1847: *Vale*—My oddities were never designed—effect of an uncalculating constitution at first, then through isolation.' 'To live to give pain rather than pleasure (the latter so delicious) seems the spider-like necessity of my being on earth, and I have gone on my queer way with joy, saying, "Shall the clay interrogate?"'

When Mrs Thoreau called on her one day, wearing pink ribbons, she shut her eyes, and so conversed with her for a time. By and by she said, 'Mrs Thoreau, I don't know whether you have observed that my eyes are shut.' 'Yes, Madam, I have observed it.' 'Perhaps you would like to know the reasons?' 'Yes, I should.' 'I don't like to see a person of your age guilty of such levity in dress.'

She was no whistle that every mouth could play on, but quite a clannish instrument, a pibroch, for example, from which none but a native Highlander could draw music.

In her solitude of twenty years, with fewest books and those only sermons, and a copy of Paradise Lost, without covers or title-page, so that later, when she heard much of Milton and sought his work, she found it was her very book which she knew so well,—she was driven to find Nature her companion and solace. She speaks of 'her attempts in Malden, to wake up the soul amid the dreary scenes of monotonous Sabbaths, when Nature looked like a pulpit.' 'But in dead of night, nearer morning, when the eastern stars glow or appear to glow with more indescribable lustre, a lustre which penetrates the spirit with wonder and curiosity—then, however awed, who can fear?'

'Folly follows me as the shadow does the form.' 'True, I must finger the very farthing candle-ends—the duty assigned to my pride. Could I but dare it on the bread-and-water diet! Could I but live free from calculation, as in the first half of life, when my poor aunt lived. I had but ten dollars a year for clothes and charity, and I never remember to have been needy.'

To her nephew Charles: 'War; what do I think of it? Why in your ear I think it so much better than oppression that if it were ravaging the whole geography of despotism it would be an omen of high and glorious import. Channing paints its miseries, but does he know those of a worse war—private animosities, pinching, bitter warfare of the human heart, the cruel oppression of the poor by the rich, which corrupts old worlds? How much better, more honest, are storming and conflagration of towns! They are but letting blood which corrupts into worms and dragons. War devastates the conscience of men, yet corrupt peace does not less.'

'O Time! Thou loiterer. Thou, whose might has laid low the vastest and crushed the worm, restest on thy hoary throne, with like potency over thy agitations and thy graves. Hasten to finish thy motley work, on which frightful Gorgons are at play, spite of holy ghosts. 'Tis already moth-eaten, and its shuttles quaver, and the beams of the loom are shaken.'

'Yet there is sombre music in the whirl of times so long gone by. And the bare bones of this poor embryo earth may give the idea of the Infinite far, far better than when dignified with arts and industry:—its ocean, when beating the symbols of ceaseless ages, than when covered with cargoes of war and oppression.'

For years she had her bed made in the form of a coffin; and delighted herself with the discovery of the figure of a coffin made every evening on their sidewalk, by the shadow of a church tower which adjoined the house.

Saladin caused his shroud to be made, and carried it into battle as his standard. She made up her shroud, and death still refusing to come, and she thinking it a pity to let it lie idle, wore it as a nightgown, or a day-gown, nay, went out to ride in it, on horseback, in her mountain roads, until it was worn out. Then she had another made up, and as she never travelled without being provided for this dear and indispensable contingency, I believe she wore out a great many.

RALPH WALDO EMERSON
From *Lectures and Biographical Sketches, 1883*. Quoted from an address, *Amita*, read before the Woman's Club, Boston, 1869, by Moody Emerson's nephew.

2   *The Sea*

Upon river, creek, and bay they are busy transforming the crude forest into staunch and gallant vessels. From every inlet or indenture along the rocky shore swim forth these ocean birds—born in the wild wood, fledged upon the wave.

It is upon the unstable element that the sons of New England have achieved their greatest triumphs. Their adventurous prows vex the waters of every sea. Bold and restless as the old northern Vikings, they go forth to seek their fortunes in the mighty deep. The ocean is their pasture, and over its wide prairies they follow the monstrous herds that feed upon its azure fields. As the hunter casts his lasso upon the wild horse, so they throw their lines into the tumbling whale. They 'draw out Leviathan with a hook.' They 'fill his skin with barbed irons,' and inspite of his terrible strength they 'part him among the merchants.' To them there are no pillars of Hercules. They seek with avidity new regions, and fear not to be 'the first that ever burst' into unknown seas.

SEARGENT SMITH PRENTISS
'An Address to the New England Society of New Orleans,' quoted by G. L. Prentiss in *A Memoir of S. S. Prentiss*, New York, 1855.

The Sea

Advice to a Boy Going to Sea:

Always go straight forward, and if you meet the Devil, cut him in two and go between the pieces; if any one imposes on you, tell him to whistle against a northwester, and to bottle up moonshine.

SEA CHANTEY: A Yankee Ship

A Yankee ship came down the river,
    Blow, boys, blow!
        Her masts and spars they shine like silver,
    Blow, my bully boys, blow!

O, what do you think that ship had in her?
    Blow, boys, blow!
        Monkeys' hides and bullocks' liver,
    Blow, my bully boys, blow!

And what do you think they had for dinner?
    Blow, boys, blow!
        Hot-water soup but slightly thinner,
    Blow, my bully boys, blow!

CARGOES UNLOADING IN SALEM HARBOR AROUND 1810:

Hemp from Luzon; pepper from Sumatra; coffee from Arabia; palm oil from the West Coast of Africa; cotton from Bombay; duck and iron from the Baltic; tallow from Madagascar; salt from Cadiz; wine from Portugal and the Madeiras; figs, raisins and almonds from the Mediterranean; teas and silks from China; sugar, rum and molasses from the West Indies; ivory and gum-copal from Zanzibar; rubber, hides and wool from South America; whale oil from the Arctic and Antarctic, and sperm from the South Seas.

Advice and *Cargoes* quoted by Ralph D. Paine, *Ships and Sailors of Old Salem,* New York, 1909.

Lord Timothy Dexter of Newburyport relates how he came to Fortune by Speculations in Warming-Pans, Whalebone, Bibles, and Government Securities

How did Dexter make his money ye says buying whale bone for staing for ships in grosing three hundred & 40 tons—bort all in boston salum and all in Noue york under Cover oppenly told them for my ships they all laffed so I had at my oan pris I had four Counning men for Rounners they found the bone as I told them to act the fool I was full of Cash I had nine tun of silver on hand at that time— all that time the Creaters laffing it spread very fast here is the Rub—in fifty days they smelt a Rat—found where it was gone to Nouebry Port—spekkelators swarmed like hell houns—to be short with it I made sevintey five per sent— one tun and halfe of silver on hand and over—one more spect—Drole a Nuf—I dreamed of worming pans three nites that thay would doue in the west inges I got no more than fortey two thousand—put them in nine vessels for different ports that tuck good hold I cleared sevinty nine per sent the pans thay made yous of them for Coucking—very good masser for Coukey—blessed good in Deade missey got nice handel Now burn my fase the best thing I Ever seen in borne days I found I was very luckky in spekklation. I Dreamed that the good book was Run Down in this countrey nine years gone so low as halfe prise and Dull at that—the bibel I means I had the Ready Cash by holl sale I bort twelve per sent under halfe pris thay Cost fortey one sents Each bibbel—twenty one thousand—I put them into twenty one vessels for the west inges and sent a text that all of them must have one bibel in every familey or if not thay would goue to hell—and if thay had Dun wiked flie to the bibel and on thare Neas and kiss the bibel three times and look up to heaven annest for forgivness my Captteins all had Compleat order—here Comes the good luck I made one hundred per sent & littel over then I found I had made money anuf I hant spekalated since old time by government secourities I made or cleared forty seven thousands Dolors—that is the old afare Now I toald the all the sekrett Now be still let me A lone Dont wonder Noe more houe I got my money boaz—

A Pickle for the Knowing Ones, Salem, 1802.

Fifteen of the Clipper Ships Built in New England 1850-1854. Together With Some of the Voyages in Which They Set Records Never Again to be Equalled by Vessels Under Sail Alone.

PLACE:	BUILDER:	SHIP:	MASTER:	VOYAGE:
Maine				
Damariscotta	Metcalf & Norris	*Flying Scud*, 1853	Warren Bearse	Day's run, 1854: 449 nautical miles claimed. *The Record?*
Rockland	Deacon George Thomas	*Red Jacket*, 1853	Asa Eldridge	New York to Liverpool, 1854: 13 days, 1 hour, 25 minutes, dock to dock. *The Record*
New Hampshire				
Portsmouth	George Raynes	*Wild Pigeon*, 1851	P. N. Mayhew	Talcahuana to New York, 1860: 50 days. *The Record*
"	" "	*Witch of the Wave*, 1851	Benjamin Tay	Calcutta to Boston, 1851: 81 days. *The Record*
Massachusetts				
Amesbury	Unknown	Bark, *Wildfire*, 1853	Mosman	Boston to Gibraltar, 1853: 14 days. *The Record*
East Boston	Donald McKay	*Flying Cloud*, 1851	Josiah Cressy	New York to Hong Kong, via San Francisco, 1851: 126 days. *The Record*
" "	" "	*Great Republic*, 1853	Joseph Limeburner	New York to Equator, 1856: 15 days, 9 hours. *The Record*
" "	" "	*James Baines*, 1854	Charles McDonnell	Liverpool to Melbourne, 1854: 63 days. *The Record*
" "	" "	*Lightning*, 1854	James Forbes	Day's run, 1854: 436 nautical miles. *The Record*
" "	Samuel Hall	Bark, *Mermaid*, 1851	Unknown	Coast of China to Golden Gate, 1853: 30 days.
" "	" "	" "	"	Shanghai to San Francisco, 1865: 31 days. *The Record*
" "	" "	*Wizard*, 1853	Woodside	Manilla to New York, 1861: 84 days. *The Record*
South Boston	E. & H. O. Briggs	*Northern Light*, 1851	Freeman Hatch	San Francisco to Boston, 1854: 76 days, 6 hours. *The Record*
" "	" "	*Meteor*, 1852	Thomas Melville	50 South Pacific to Equator, 1859. 15½ days. *The Record*
Chelsea	Paul Curtis	*Witchcraft*, 1850	William Rogers	Rio de Janeiro to San Francisco, 1851: 62 days. *The Record*
Connecticut				
Mystic	Irons & Grinnell	*Andrew Jackson*, 1855	John Williams	New York to San Francisco, 1860: 89 days, 4 hours. *The Record*

Compiled from Carl C. Cutler, *Greyhounds of the Sea*, 1930.

FURLING SAIL OFF CAPE HORN

It came on to blow worse and worse, with hail and snow beating like so many furies upon the ship, it being as dark and thick as night could make it. The mainsail was blowing and slatting with a noise like thunder, when the captain came on deck and ordered it to be furled. The mate was about to call all hands when the captain stopped him, and said that the men would be beaten out if they were called up so often; that, as our watch must stay on deck, it might as well be doing that as anything else.

Accordingly, we went upon the yard; and never shall I forget that piece of work. Our watch had been so reduced by sickness, and by some having been left in California, that, with one man at the wheel, we had only the third mate and three besides myself to go aloft; so that at most we could only attempt to furl one yard-arm at a time.

We manned the weather yard-arm, and set to work to make a furl of it. The yard over which we lay was cased with ice, the gaskets and rope of the foot and leech of the sail as stiff and hard as a piece of leather hose, and the sail itself about as pliable as though it had been made of sheathing copper. We had to *fist* the sail with bare hands. No one could trust himself to mittens, for if he slipped he was a gone man. All the boats were hoisted in on deck, and there was nothing to be lowered for him. We had need of every finger God had given us.

Several times we got the sail upon the yard, but it blew away again before we could secure it. Frequently we were obliged to leave off altogether and take to beating our hands upon the sail to keep them from freezing. After some time—which seemed for ever—we got the weather side stowed after a fashion, and went over to leeward for another trial. This was still worse, for the body of the sail had been blown over to leeward. When the yard-arms were furled, the bunt was all adrift again, which made more work for us. We got all secure at last, but we had been nearly an hour and a half upon the yard, and it seemed an age. It had just struck five bells when we went up, and eight were struck soon after we came down.

We were glad enough to get on deck, and still more to go down. The oldest sailor in the watch said, as he went down, 'I shall never forget that mainyard; it beats all my going a-fishing. Fun is fun, but furling one yard-arm of a course at a time, off Cape Horn, is no better than man-killing.'

Tuesday evening [December 12, 1850] Pittsfield, Mass.

I have a sort of sea-feeling here in the country, now that the ground is all covered with snow. I look out of my window in the morning when I rise, as I would out of a porthole of a ship in the Atlantic. My room seems a ship's cabin; and at night when I wake up and hear the wind shrieking, I almost fancy there is too much sail on the house, and I had better go on the roof and rig the chimney.

RICHARD HENRY DANA JR.
Two Years Before the Mast, New York, 1840.

HERMAN MELVILLE
Letter to Evert Duyckinck.

The Sea

It was a sight full of quick wonder and awe! The vast swells of the omnipotent sea; the surging, hollow roar they made, as they rolled along the eight gunwales, like gigantic bowls in a boundless bowling-green; the brief suspended agony of the boat, as it would tip for an instant on the knife-like edge of the sharper waves, that almost seemed threatening to cut it in two; the sudden profound dip into the watery glens and hollows; the keen spurrings and goadings to gain the top of the opposite hill; the headlong, sled-like slide down its other side;—all these, with the cries of the headsmen and harpooners, and the shuddering gasps of the oarsmen, with the wondrous sight of the ivory Pequod bearing down upon her boats with outstretched sails, like a wild hen after her screaming brood;—all this was thrilling. Not the raw recruit, marching from the bosom of his wife into the fever heat of his first battle; not the dead man's ghost encountering the first unknown phantom in the other world;—neither of these can feel stranger and stronger emotions than that man does, who for the first time finds himself pulling into the charmed, churned circle of the hunted sperm whale.

The dancing white water made by the chase was now becoming more and more visible, owing to the increasing darkness of the dun cloud-shadows flung upon the sea. The jets of vapor no longer blended, but tilted everywhere to right and left; the whales seemed separating their wakes. The boats were pulled more apart; Starbuck giving chase to three whales running dead to leeward. Our sail was now set, and, with the still rising wind, we rushed along; the boat going with such madness through the water, that the lee oars could scarcely be worked rapidly enough to escape being torn from the row-locks.

Soon we were running through a suffusing wide veil of mist; neither ship nor boat to be seen.

'Give way, men,' whispered Starbuck, drawing still further aft the sheet of his sail; 'there is time to kill a fish yet before the squall comes. There's white water again—close to! Spring!'

Soon after, two cries in quick succession on each side of us denoted that the other boats had got fast; but hardly were they overheard, when with a lightning-like hurtling whisper Starbuck said: 'Stand up!' and Queepueg, harpoon in hand, sprang to his feet.

Though not one of the oarsmen was then facing the life and death peril so close to them ahead, yet with their eyes on the intense countenance of the mate in the stern of the boat, they knew that the imminent instant had come; they heard, too, an enormous wallowing sound as of fifty elephants stirring in their litter. Meanwhile the boat was still booming through the mist, the waves curling and hissing around us like the erected crests of enraged serpents.

'That's his hump. *There, there,* give it to him!' whispered Starbuck.

A short rushing sound leaped out of the boat; it was the darted iron of Queepueg. Then all in one welded commotion came an invisible push from astern, while forward the boat seemed striking on a ledge; the sail collapsed and exploded; a gush of scalding vapor shot up near by; something rolled and tumbled like an earthquake beneath us. The whole crew were half suffocated as they were tossed helter-skelter into the white curdling cream of the squall. Squall, whale, and harpoon had all blended together; and the whale, merely grazed by the iron, escaped.

HERMAN MELVILLE
Moby Dick, or the Whale, New York, 1851.

THE WHALE SHIP ESSEX

I. *The wreck*

The ship *Essex*, Captain George Pollard, sailed from Nantucket, 1819, on a whaling voyage to the Pacific Ocean.

On the 20th of the 11th month, 1820, a school of whales was discovered, and in pursuing them the mate's boat was stove, which obliged him to return to the ship. The captain and 2nd mate were left with their boats pursuing the whales. The mate discovered a large spermaceti whale near the ship, but it gave them no alarm, until they saw the whale coming at full speed towards them. In a moment they were astonished by a tremendous crash. The whale had struck the ship a little forward of the fore chains.

It was some minutes before the crew could recover from their astonishment. They then tried their pumps, and found that the ship was sinking. A signal was immediately set for the boats. The whale now appeared again making for the ship and, coming with great velocity, he struck the ship a second blow, which nearly stove in her bows. There was now no hope of saving the ship. They collected a few things, hove them into the boat, and shoved off. The ship immediately fell upon one side and sunk to the water's edge. When the captain's and 2nd mate's boats arrived, such was the consternation, that for some time not a word was spoken. The danger of their situation at length aroused them, as from a terrific dream, to a no less terrific reality.

They cut away the masts, which caused her to right a little. Holes were then cut in the deck, by which they obtained about 600 pounds of bread, and as much water as they could take, besides other articles likely to be of use to them. On the 22nd of 11 month, they left the ship, with as gloomy a prospect before them as can well be imagined. The nearest land was about 1,000 miles to the windward of them; they were in open boats, weak and leaky, with a very small pittance of bread and water for the support of so many men.

II. *Survivors in the mate's boat*

Isaac Cole, one of our crew, had the day before this, in a fit of despair, thrown himself down in the boat, and was determined there calmly to wait for death. All was dark, he said, in his mind, not a single ray of hope was left for him to dwell upon; and it was folly and madness to be struggling against what appeared so palpably to be our fixed and settled destiny. I remonstrated with him as effectually as the weakness both of my body and understanding would allow of; and what I said appeared for a moment to have a considerable effect: he made a powerful and sudden effort, half rose up, crawled forward and hoisted the jib, and firmly and loudly cried that he would live as long as the rest of us—but alas! the effort was but the hectic fever of the moment, and he shortly again relapsed into a state of melancholy and despair. This day his reason was attacked, and he became about 9 o'clock a most miserable spectacle of madness: he spoke incoherently about everything, calling loudly for a napkin and water, and then lying stupidly and senselessly down in the boat again, would close his hollow eyes, as if in death.

About 10 o'clock, we suddenly perceived that he became speechless; we got him as well as we were able upon a board placed on one of the seats of the boat, and covering him up with some old clothes, left him to his fate. He lay in the greatest pain and apparent misery, groaning piteously until 4 o'clock, when he died, in the most horrid and frightful convulsions I ever witnessed.

We kept his corpse all night, and in the morning my two companions began as of course to make preparations to dispose of it in the sea; when after reflecting on the subject all night, I addressed them on the painful subject of keeping the body for food!! Our provisions could not possibly last us beyond three days, within which time it was not in any degree probable that we should find relief from our present sufferings, and that hunger would at last drive us to the necessity of casting lots. It was without any objection agreed to, and we set to work as fast as we were able to prepare it so as to prevent its spoiling. We separated his limbs from his body, and cut all the flesh from the bones; after which we opened the body, took out the heart and then closed it again—sewed it up as decently as we could and committed it to the sea. The heart we eagerly devoured, and then eat sparingly of a few pieces of the flesh; after which we hung up the remainder, cut in thin strips, about the boat to dry in the sun; we made a fire and roasted some of it, to serve us during the next day. We knew not then to whose lot it would fall next, either to die or be shot, and eaten like the poor wretch we had just despatched. Humanity must shudder at the dreadful recital. I have not language to paint the anguish of our souls in this dreadful dilemma.

On the sixteenth, at night, full of the horrible reflections of our situation, and panting with weakness, I laid down to sleep, almost indifferent whether I should ever see the light again. I had not lain long before I dreamt I saw a ship at some distance off from us, and strained every nerve to get to her, but could not. I awoke almost overpowered with the frenzy I had caught in my slumbers, and stung with the cruelties of a diseased and disappointed imagination.

The next morning, at about 7 o'clock, my companion who was steering suddenly and loudly called out, *'There's a sail!'* Immediately I stood up, gazing in a state of abstraction and ecstacy upon the blessed vision of a vessel about seven miles off; she was standing in the same direction with us, and the only sensation I felt at the moment was that of a violent impulse to fly directly towards her. Upon observing us, she shortened sail and allowed us to come up to her. The captain hailed us and asked who we were. I told him we were from a wreck. Our cadaverous countenances, sunken eyes, and bones just starting through the skin, with the ragged remnants of clothes stuck about our sunburnt bodies, must have produced an appearance affecting and revolting in the highest degree. The sailors commenced to remove us from our boat, and we were taken to the cabin. In a few minutes we were permitted to taste a little thin food, made from tapioca.

OBED MACY
The History of Nantucket, Boston, 1835.

OWEN CHASE, FIRST MATE
Narrative of the Most Extraordinary and Distressing Shipwreck of the Whale Ship Essex, New York, 1821.

Prayers for Salem

Sunday, April 24, 1785.

Notes for Hannah Hodgdon, sick and brother at sea.
Hannah Bushnel, for sister's death and brother at sea.
Hannah Archer, death of daughter and friend at sea.
Mary Whitford, death of sister and friend at sea.
David Newhall, sick and son at sea.

August 13.

Mary Lauchlin, delivery, and husband at sea.
Martha Gale, death of husband and brother at sea.
Mary Crowninshield, death of son-in-law, and sons at sea.

July 3, 1791.

Anna Bowditch, death of husband, and prayer for her brethren at sea.
Mary Batten, sudden death of her only son and for son-in-law at sea.
Sarah Batten, sudden death of her husband, and prayer for brethren at sea.
Elizabeth Cotton, death of her brother, and for her husband and brother at sea.
Elizabeth Mason, death of youngest child and prayer for husband and friends at sea.
Preserved Elkins returns thanks for the remarkable
preservation of her husband, asks prayers for his safe
return and for absent brethren.

THE REVEREND WILLIAM BENTLEY
Ships and Sailors of Old Salem, 1909.

Full Sail

Notwithstanding all that has been said about the beauty of a ship under full sail, there are very few who have ever seen a ship, literally, under all her sail. A ship coming in or going out of port, with her ordinary sails, and perhaps two or three studding sails, is commonly said to be under full sail; but a ship never has all her sail upon her except when she has a light steady breeze, very nearly but not quite dead aft, and so regular that it can be trusted and is likely to last for some time.

Then, with all her sails, on each side, alow and aloft, she is the most glorious moving object in the world. Such a sight very few, even some who have been to sea a good deal, have ever beheld; for from the deck of your own vessel you cannot see her as you would a separate object.

One night, while we were in the tropics, I went out to the end of the flying jib boom upon some duty, and lay over the boom a long time, admiring the beauty of the sight before me. Being so far out from the deck, I could look at the ship as at a separate vessel; and there rose up from the water, supported only by the small black hull, a pyramid of canvas, spreading out far beyond the hull, and towering up almost, as it seemed in the indistinct night air, to the clouds.

The sea was as still as an inland lake; the light trade-wind was gently and steadily breathing from astern; the dark blue sky was studded with the tropical stars; there was no sound but the rippling of the water under the stem; and the sails were spread out wide and high—the two lower studding sails stretching out on each side far beyond the deck; the topmast studding sails spreading fearlessly out above them; still higher, the two royal studding sails looking like two kites from the same string; and highest of all, the little sky sail, the apex of the pyramid, seeming actually to touch the stars, and to be out of reach of human hand.

So quiet too was the sea, and so steady the breeze, that if these sails had been sculptured marble they could not have been more motionless. Not a ripple upon the surface of the canvas; not even a quivering of the extreme edges of the sail; so perfectly were they distended by the breeze.

I was so lost in the sight that I forgot the presence of the man who came out with me, until he said (for he, too, rough old man-of-war's man as he was, had been gazing at the show) half to himself, still looking at the marble sails—'How quietly they do their work!'

RICHARD HENRY DANA JR.
Two Years Before the Mast, New York, 1840.

3   *Fine Auroras*

It is much to know that poetry has been written this very day, under this roof, by your side. What! that wonderful spirit has not yet expired! These stony moments are still sparkling and animated! I had fancied that the oracles were all silent, and nature had spent her fires; and behold! all night, from every pore, these fine auroras have been streaming!

RALPH WALDO EMERSON
'The Poet,' *Essays, Second Series*, Boston, 1854.

Fine Auroras

October 18, 1839

Adam in The Garden, I am to new name all the beasts in the field, and all the gods in the sky. I am to invite men drenched in time to recover themselves and come out of time, and taste their native immortal air. I am to fire with what skill I can the artillery of sympathy and emotion. I am to indicate constantly, though all unworthy, the Ideal and Holy Life, the life within life, the Forgotten Good, the Unknown Cause in which we sprawl and sin. I am to try the magic of sincerity, that luxury permitted only to kings and poets. I am to celebrate the spiritual powers in their infinite contrast to the mechanical powers and the mechanical philosophy of this time.

Morning brings back the heroic ages. I was as much affected by the faint hum of a mosquito making its invisible and unimaginable tour through my apartment at earliest dawn, when I was sitting with doors and windows open, as I could be by any trumpet that ever sang of fame. It was Homer's requiem; itself an Iliad and Odyssey in the air, singing its own wrath and wanderings. There was something cosmical about it; a standing advertisement, till forbidden, of the everlasting vigor and fertility of the world.

The morning wind forever blows, the poem of creation is uninterrupted; but few are the ears that hear it. Olympus is but the outside of the earth everywhere.

Morning work! By the blushes of Aurora and the music of Memnon, what should be man's *morning work* in this world? I had three pieces of limestone on my desk, but I was terrified to find that they required to be dusted daily, when the furniture of my mind was all undusted still, and I threw them out of the window in disgust.

The light which puts out our eyes is darkness to us. Only that day dawns to which we are awake. There is more day to dawn. The sun is but a morning star.

RALPH WALDO EMERSON
Journal.

HENRY DAVID THOREAU
Walden, Boston, 1854.

Walden Pond

Standing on the smooth sandy beach at the east end of the pond, in a calm September afternoon, when a slight haze makes the opposite shore-line indistinct, I have seen whence came the expression, 'the glassy surface of a lake.' When you invert your head, it looks like a thread of the finest gossamer stretched across the valley, and gleaming against the distant pine woods, separating one stratum of the atmosphere from another. You would think that you could walk dry under it to the opposite hills, and that the swallows which skim over might perch on it. Indeed, they sometimes dive below the line, as it were by mistake, and are undeceived.

As you look over the pond westward, you are obliged to employ both your hands to defend your eyes against the reflected as well as the true sun, for they are equally bright; and if, between the two, you survey its surface critically, it is literally as smooth as glass, except where the skater insects, at equal distances scattered over its whole extent, by their motions produce the finest imaginable sparkle on it, or, perchance, a duck plumes itself, or, as I have said, a swallow skims so low as to touch it.

It may be that in the distance a fish describes an arc of three or four feet in the air, and there is a bright flash where it emerges, and another where it strikes the water; sometimes the whole silvery arc is revealed, or here and there, perhaps, is a thistle-down floating on its surface, which the fishes dart at and so dimple it again. It is like molten glass cooled but not congealed, and the few motes in it are pure and beautiful like the imperfections in glass.

How peaceful the phenomena of the lake! Again the works of man shine as in the spring. Ay, every leaf and twig and stone and cobweb sparkles now at mid-afternoon as when covered with dew on a spring morning. Every motion of an oar or an insect produces a flash of light; and if an oar falls, how sweet the echo!

HENRY DAVID THOREAU
Walden, Boston, 1854.

Hummingbird

A route of evanescence
With a revolving wheel;
A resonance of emerald,
A rush of cochineal;
And every blossom on the bush
Adjusts its tumbled head,—
The mail from Tunis, probably,
An easy morning's ride.

Cocoon

Drab habitation of whom?
Tabernacle or tomb,
Or dome of worm,
Or porch of gnome,
Or some elf's catacomb?

EMILY DICKINSON
Poems, Second Series, Boston, 1891.
Poems, Third Series, Boston, 1896.

To Sophia

Boston, March 15, 1840

My heart is heavy: or, no, it is not heaviness,—not the heaviness like a great lump of ice, which I used to feel when I was alone in the world,—but—but—in short, dearest, where you are not, there is a sort of death,—a death, however, in which there is still hope, and assurance of a joyful life to come. Methinks, if my spirit were not conscious of yours, this dreary snow-storm would chill me to torpor; the warmth of my fireside would be quite powerless to counteract it.

Boston, October, 1840

Sometimes, during my solitary life in our old Salem house, it seemed to me as if I had only life enough to know that I was not alive; for I had no wife then to keep my heart warm. But, at length, you were revealed to me, in the shadow of a seclusion as deep as my own. I drew nearer and nearer to you, and you came to me, and will remain forever, keeping my heart warm and renewing my life with your own. You only have taught me that I have a heart,—you only have thrown a light, deep downward and upward, into my soul. You only have revealed me to myself; for without your aid my best knowledge of myself would have been merely to know my own shadow,—to watch it flickering on the wall, and mistake its fantasies for my own real actions.

Salem, Sept. 3, 1841

I have been out only once, in the daytime, since my arrival. How immediately and irrecoverably (if you did not keep me out of the abyss) should I relapse into the way of life in which I spent my youth! If it were not for you, this present world would see no more of me forever. The sunshine would fall on me, no more than on a ghost. Once in a while people might discern my figure gliding stealthily through the dim evening,—that would be all. I should be only a shadow of the night; it is you that give me reality, and make all things real for me. If, in the intervals since I quitted this lonely old chamber, I had found no woman (and you were the only possible one) to impart reality and significance to life, I should have come back hither ere now, with a feeling that all was a dream and a mockery. Do you rejoice that you have saved me from such a fate? Yes; it is a miracle worthy even of you, to have converted a life of shadows into the deepest truth by your magic touch.

Salem, June 20, 1842

Nothing can part us now; God himself hath ordained that we shall be one. So nothing remains but to reconcile yourself to your destiny. Year by year we shall grow closer to each other; and a thousand ages hence, we shall be only in the honeymoon of our marriage. But I cannot write to you. The time for that species of communion is past.

NATHANIEL HAWTHORNE
Letters to his future wife, 1840-42.

NOTE-BOOK

In an old house, a mysterious knocking might be heard on the wall, where had formerly been a doorway, now bricked up.

Cannon transformed to church-bells.

A ghost seen by moonlight; when the moon was out, it would shine and melt through the airy substance of the ghost, as through a cloud.

The scene of a story or sketch to be laid within the light of a street lantern; the time, when the lamp is near going out; and the catastrophe to be simultaneous with the last flickering gleam.

A recluse, like myself, or a prisoner, to measure time by the progress of sunshine through his chamber.

Some moderns to build a fire on Ararat with the remnant of the ark.

To have ice in one's blood.

The semblance of a human face to be formed on the side of a mountain, or in the fracture of a small stone, by a *lusus naturae*. The face is an object of curiosity for years or centuries, and by and by a boy is born, whose features gradually assume the aspect of that portrait. At some critical juncture, the resemblance is found to be perfect. A prophecy may be connected.

A man to swallow a small snake,—and it to be a symbol of a cherished sin.

To trace out the influence of a frightful and disgraceful crime in debasing and destroying a character naturally high and noble, the guilty person being alone conscious of the crime.

A man, unknown, conscious of temptation to secret crimes, puts up a note in church, desiring the prayers of the congregation for one so tempted.

The ideas of people in general are not raised higher than the roofs of the houses. All their interests extend over the earth's surface in a layer of that thickness. The meeting-house steeple reaches out of their sphere.

A stray leaf from the book of fate, picked up in the street.

The print in blood of a naked foot to be traced through the street of a town.

NATHANIEL HAWTHORNE

MARGARET FULLER

A man's ambition, with a woman's heart, is an evil lot.

For all the tides of life that flow within me, I am dumb and ineffectual, when it comes to casting my thought into a form. No old one suits me. If I could invent one, it seems to me the pleasure of creation would make it possible for me to write. What shall I do, dear friend? I want force to be either a genius or a character. One should be either private or public. I love best to be a woman; but womanhood is at present too straitly-bound to give me scope. At hours, I live truly as a woman; at others, I should stifle.

I have known some happy hours, but they all lead to sorrow, and not only the cups of wine, but of milk, seem drugged with poison, for me. It does not seem to be my fault, this destiny. I do not court these things,—they come. I am a poor magnet, with power to be wounded by the bodies I attract.

In the chamber of death, I prayed in very early years, 'Give me the truth; cheat me by no illusion.' O, the granting of this prayer is sometimes terrible to me! I walk over the burning ploughshares, and they sear my feet. Yet nothing but truth will do; no love will serve that is not eternal, and as large as the universe; no philanthropy in executing whose behests I myself become unhealthy; no creative genius which burst asunder my life, to leave it a poor black chrysalid behind. And yet this last is too true of me.

Quoted by Ralph Waldo Emerson, 'Visits to Concord,' in *Memoirs of Margaret Fuller Ossoli*, vol. I, Boston, 1852.

MARTHA HUNT

NOTE: In *The Blithedale Romance,* based on his experiences at Brook Farm, Hawthorne modeled his chief character, Zenobia, after Margaret Fuller. Margaret was drowned in a shipwreck: Zenobia drowned herself. The search for her body is founded on the following passage from his journal.

Concord, 1845

On the night of July 9th a search for the dead body of a drowned girl.—She was a Miss Hunt, about nineteen years old; a girl of education and refinement, but depressed and miserable for want of sympathy—her family being an affectionate one, but uncultivated, and incapable of responding to her demands. She was of melancholic temperament, accustomed to solitary walks in the woods. At this time, she had the superintendence of one of the district schools, comprising sixty scholars, particularly difficult of management. Well, Ellery Channing knocked at the door between 9 and 10 in the evening, in order to get my boat to go in search of this girl's drowned body. He took the oars, and I the paddle, and we went rapidly down the river, until, a good distance below the bridge, we saw lights on the bank, and the dim figures of a number of people waiting for us. Her bonnet and shoes had already been found on this spot, and her handkerchief, I believe, on the edge of the water; so that the body was probably at no great distance, unless the current (which is gentle and almost imperceptible) had swept her down.

We took in General Buttrick, and a young man in a blue frock, and commenced the search; the General and the other man having long poles, with hooks at the end, and Ellery a hayrake, while I steered the boat. It was a very eligible place to drown one's self. On the verge of the river, there were water-weeds; but after a few steps, the bank goes off very abruptly, and the water speedily becomes fifteen or twenty feet deep. It must be one of the deepest spots in the whole river; and, holding a lantern over it, it was black as midnight, smooth, impenetrable, and keeping its secrets from the eye as perfectly as mid-ocean could. . . . Once or twice the pole or the rake caught in bunches of water-weed, which, in the starlight, looked like garments; and once Ellery and the General struck some substance at the bottom, which they at first mistook for the body; but it was probably a sod that had rolled in from the bank. I now paddled the boat again past the point where she was supposed to have entered the river, and then turned it, so as to let it float broadside downwards, about midway from bank to bank. The young fellow in the blue frock sat on the next seat to me, plying his long pole.

We had drifted a little distance below the group of men on the bank, when the fellow gave a sudden start. 'What's this?' cried he. I felt in an instant what it was; and I suppose the same electric shock went through everybody in the boat. 'Yes; I've got her!' said he; and heaving up his pole with difficulty, there was an appearance of light garments on the surface of the water. He made a strong effort, and brought so much of the body above the surface, that there could be no doubt about it. He drew her towards the boat, grasped her arm or hand; and I steered the boat to the bank, all the while looking at the dead girl, whose limbs were swaying in the water, close at the boat's side. The fellow evidently had the same sort of feeling in his success as if he had caught a particularly fine fish; though mingled, no doubt, with horror. For my own part, I felt my voice tremble a little, when I spoke, at the first shock of the discovery; and at seeing the body come close to the surface, dimly in the starlight. When close to the bank, some of the men stepped into the water and drew out the body; and then, by their lanterns, I could see how rigid it was.... They took her out of the water, and deposited her under an oak-tree; and by the time we had got ashore, they were examining her by the light of two or three lanterns.

I never saw nor imagined a spectacle of such perfect horror. Her arms had stiffened in the act of struggling; and were bent before her, with the hands clenched. She was the very image of a death-agony; and when the men tried to compose her figure, her arms would still return to that same position; indeed it was almost impossible to force them out of it for an instant. One of the men put his foot upon her arm, for the purpose of reducing it by her side; but in a moment, it rose again. The lower part of the body had stiffened into a more quiet attitude; the legs were slightly bent; and the feet close together. But that rigidity! —it is impossible to express the effect of it; it seemed as if she would keep the same posture in the grave, and that her skeleton would keep it too, and that when she rose at the day of judgment, it would be in the same attitude.

As soon as she was taken out of the water, the blood began to stream from her nose. Two of the men got water, and began to wash away the blood from her face; but it flowed and flowed, and continued to flow; and an old carpenter, who seemed to be skillful in such matters, said that this was always the case, and that she would continue to 'purge,' as he called it, in this manner until her burial.

A young brother of the deceased, apparently about twelve or fourteen years old, had been on the spot from the beginning. He seemed not much moved, externally, but answered questions about his sister, and the number of the brothers and sisters (ten in all), with composure. No doubt, however, he was stunned and bewildered with the scene—to see his sister lying there, in such terrific guise, at midnight, under an oak, on the verge of the black river, with strangers clustering about her, holding their lanterns over her face; and that old carpenter washing the blood away, which still flowed, though from a frozen fountain. All the while, we were talking about the circumstances, and about an inquest, and whether or not it was necessary, and of how many it should consist; and the old carpenter was talking of dead people, and how he would as lief handle them as living ones.

By this time, two rails had been procured, across which were laid some boards, or broken oars from the bottom of a boat; and the body, being wrapt in an old quilt, was laid upon this rude bier. All of us took part in bearing the corpse, or in steadying it. From the bank of the river to her father's house, there was nearly half a mile of pasture-ground, on the ascent of the hill; and our burthen grew very heavy, before we reached the door. What a midnight procession it was! How strange and fearful it would have seemed, if it could have been foretold, a day beforehand, that I should help carry a dead body along that track! At last, we reached the door, where appeared an old gray-haired man, holding a light; he said nothing, seemed calm, and after the body was laid upon a large table, in what seemed to be the kitchen, the old man disappeared.

NATHANIEL HAWTHORNE

Fine Auroras

Not with a club the heart is broken,
Nor with a stone;
A whip, so small you could not see it,
I've known

To lash the magic creature
Till it fell,
Yet that whip's name too noble
Then to tell.

Magnanimous of bird
By boy descried
To sing unto the stone
Of which it died.

*   *   *   *   *

The heart asks pleasure first,
And then, excuse from pain;
And then, those little anodynes
That deaden suffering;

And then, to go to sleep;
And then, if it should be
The will of its Inquisitor
The liberty to die.

EMILY DICKINSON
Poems, Third Series, Boston, 1896.
Poems, Boston, 1890.

Pittsfield, Massachusetts, 1851
My Dear Hawthorne,—
I should have been rumbling down to you in my pine-board chariot a long time ago, were it not that for some weeks past I have been building and patching and tinkering away in all directions. Besides, I had my crops to get in,—corn and potatoes. But I mean to continue visiting you until you tell me that my visits are both derogatory and superfluous.

With no son of man do I stand upon any etiquette or ceremony, except the Christian ones of charity and honesty. I am told, my fellowman, that there is an aristocracy of the brain. Some men have boldly advocated and asserted it. Schiller seems to have done so, though I don't know much about him. At any rate, it is true that there have been those who, while earnest about political equality, still accept the intellectual estates. And I can well perceive, I think, how a man of superior mind can, by its intense cultivation, bring himself, as it were, into a certain spontaneous aristocracy of feeling,—exceedingly nice and fastidious,—similar to that which, in an English Howard, conveys a torpedo-fish thrill at the slightest contact with a social plebian. So, when you see or hear of my ruthless democracy on all sides, you may possibly feel a touch of a shrink, or something of that sort. It is but nature to be shy of a mortal who boldly asserts that a thief in jail is as honorable a personage as Gen. George Washington.

This is ludicrous. But Truth is the silliest thing under the sun. Try to get a living by the Truth—and go to the Soup Societies. Heavens! Let any clergyman try to preach the Truth from its very stronghold, the pulpit, and they would ride him out of his church on his own pulpit bannister. It can hardly be doubted that all Reformers are bottomed upon the Truth, more or less; and to the world at large are not reformers almost universally laughing-stocks? Why so? Truth is ludicrous to men.

In a week or so, I go to New York, to bury myself in a third-story room, and work and slave on my 'Whale' while it is driving through the press. *That* is the only way I can finish it now,—I am so pulled hither and thither by circumstances. The calm, the coolness, the silent grass-growing mood in which a man *ought* always to compose,—that, I fear, can seldom be mine. Dollars damn me; and the malicious Devil is forever grinning in upon me, holding the door ajar. What I feel most moved to write, that is banned, —it will not pay. Yet, altogether, write the *other* way I cannot. So the product is a final hash, and all my books are botches.

I'm rather sore, perhaps, in this letter; but see my hand! —four blisters on this palm, made by hoes and hammers within the last few days. It is a rainy morning; so I am indoors, and all work suspended. I feel cheerfully disposed, and therefore I write a little bluely.

If ever, my dear Hawthorne, in the eternal times that are to come, you and I shall sit down in Paradise, in some little shady corner by ourselves; and if we shall by any means be able to smuggle a basket of champagne there (I won't believe in a Temperance Heaven), and if we shall then cross our celestial legs in the celestial grass that is forever tropical, and strike our glasses and our heads together, till both musically ring in concert,—then, O my dear fellow-mortal, how shall we pleasantly discourse of all the things manifold which now so distress us,—when all the earth shall be but a reminiscence, yea, its final dissolution an antiquity. Then shall songs be composed as when wars are over; humorous, comic songs,—'Oh, when I lived in that queer little

Fine Auroras

hole called the world,' or, 'Oh, when I toiled and sweated below,' or, 'Oh, when I knocked and was knocked in the fight'—yes, let us look forward to such things. Let us swear that, though now we sweat, yet it is because of the dry heat which is indispensable to the nourishment of the vine which is to bear the grapes that are to give us the champagne hereafter.

But I was talking about the 'Whale.' As the fishermen say, 'he's in his flurry' when I left him some three weeks ago. I'm going to take him by the jaw, however, before long, and finish him up in some fashion or other. What's the use of elaborating what, in its very essence, is so short-lived as a modern book? Though I wrote the Gospels in this century, I should die in the gutter.

It is a frightful poetical creed that the cultivation of the brain eats out the heart. But it's my *prose* opinion that in most cases, in those men who have fine brains and work them well, the heart extends down to hams. And though you smoke them with the fire of tribulation, yet, like veritable hams, the head only gives the richer and the better flavor. I stand for the heart. To the dogs with the head! I had rather be a fool with a heart, than Jupiter Olympus with his head. The reason the mass of men fear God, and *at bottom dislike* Him, is because they rather distrust His heart, and fancy Him all brain like a watch. (You perceive I employ a capital initial in the pronoun referring to the Deity; don't you think there is a slight dash of flunkeyism in that usage?)

My development has been all within a few years past. I am like one of those seeds taken out of the Egyptian Pyramids, which, after being three thousand years a seed and nothing but a seed, being planted in English soil, it developed itself, grew to greenness, and then fell to mould. So I. Until I was twenty-five, I had no development at all. From my twenty-fifth year I date my life. Three weeks have scarcely passed, at any time between then and now, that I have not unfolded within myself. But I feel that I am now come to the inmost leaf of the bulb, and that shortly the flower must fall to the mould.

In reading some of Goethe's sayings, so worshipped by his votaries, I came across this, '*Live in the all.*' What nonsense! Here is a fellow with a raging toothache. 'My dear boy,' Goethe says to him, 'you are sorely afflicted with that tooth; but you must *live in the all,* and then you will be happy!' As with all great genius, there is an immense deal of flummery in Goethe, and in proportion to my own contact with him, a monstrous deal of it in me.

H. Melville

PS. 'Amen!' saith Hawthorne.

NB. This 'all' feeling, though, there is some truth in it. You must often have felt it, lying on the grass on a warm summer's day. Your legs seem to send out shoots into the earth. Your hair feels like leaves upon your head. This is the *all* feeling. But what plays the mischief with the truth is that men will insist upon the universal application of a temporary feeling or opinion.

PS. You must not fail to admire my discretion in paying the postage on this letter.

HERMAN MELVILLE
Quoted by Julian Hawthorne in *Nathaniel Hawthorne and His Wife,* Boston, 1885.

Fine Auroras

'All visible objects, man, are but as pasteboard masks. But in each event—in the living act, the undoubted deed—there, some unknown but still reasoning thing puts forth the mouldings of its features from behind the unreasoning mask. If man will strike, strike through the mask! How can the prisoner reach outside except by thrusting through the wall? To me, the white whale is that wall, shoved near to me. Sometimes I think there's naught beyond. But 'tis enough. He tasks me; he heaps me; I see in him outrageous strength, with an inscrutable malice sinewing it. That inscrutable thing is chiefly what I hate; and be the white whale agent, or be the white whale principal, I will wreak that hate upon him. Talk not to me of blasphemy, man; I'd strike the sun if it insulted me.'

HERMAN MELVILLE
Ahab to Starbuck, *Moby Dick, or the Whale,* New York, 1851.

4   *Protest*

A Born Protestant

I have travelled a good deal in Concord; and everywhere, in shops, and offices, and fields, the inhabitants have appeared to me to be doing penance in a thousand remarkable ways. How many a poor immortal soul have I met well-nigh crushed and smothered under its load, creeping down the road of life, pushing before it a barn seventy-five feet by forty, its Augean stables never cleansed, and one hundred acres of land, tillage, mowing, pasture, and wood-lot! The better part of the man is soon plowed into the soil for compost.

The mass of men lead lives of quiet desperation.

I am convinced, both by faith and experience, that to maintain one's self on this earth is not a hardship but a pastime, if we will live simply and wisely; as the pursuits of the simpler nations are still the sports of the more artificial. It is not necessary that a man should earn his living by the sweat of his brow, unless he sweats easier than I do.

HENRY DAVID THOREAU
Walden, 1854.

It is remarkable that there is little or nothing to be remembered written on the subject of getting a living; how to make getting a living not merely honest and honorable, but altogether inviting and glorious; for if *getting* a living is not, then living is not.

A man had better starve at once than lose his innocence in the process of getting his bread.

If a man walk in the woods half of each day, he is in danger of being regarded as a loafer; but if he spends his whole day as a speculator, shearing off those woods and making earth bald before her time, he is esteemed an industrious and enterprising citizen. As if a town had no interest in its forests but to cut them down!

What is it to be born free and not to live free? What is the value of any political freedom, but as a means to moral freedom? Is it a freedom to be slaves, or a freedom to be free, of which we boast.

The chief want, in every State that I have been into, was a high and earnest purpose in the inhabitants.

A very few, as heroes, patriots, martyrs, reformers in the great sense, and *men,* serve the state with their consciences also, and so necessarily resist it for the most part; and they are commonly treated as enemies by it.

What is the price-current of an honest man and patriot today? They hesitate, and they regret, and sometimes they petition; but they do nothing in earnest and with effect. They will wait, well disposed, for others to remedy the evil, that they may no longer have it to regret. At most, they give only a cheap vote, and a feeble countenance and God-speed to the right as it goes by them. If I devote myself to other pursuits and contemplations, I must first see that I do not pursue them sitting upon another man's shoulders. I must get off him first, that he may pursue his contemplations, too.

Is there not a sort of blood shed when the conscience is wounded? Through this wound a man's real manhood and immortality flow out, and he bleeds to an everlasting death. I see this blood flowing now.

The law will never make men free; it is men who have got to make the law free. They are the lovers of law and order who observe the law when the government breaks it.

HENRY DAVID THOREAU
Life without Principle, 1863, *Civil Disobedience,* 1849, and *Slavery in Massachusetts,* 1854.

Rights of Woman

For any human being or class of human beings, whether black, white, male or female, tamely to submit to the denial of their right to self-government shows that the instinct of liberty has been blotted out.

You blunder on this question of woman's rights just where thousands of others do. You believe woman unlike man in her nature; that conditions of life which any man of spirit would sooner die than accept are not only endurable to woman, but are needful to her fullest enjoyment. Make her position in church, State, marriage, your own; everywhere your equality ignored, everywhere made to feel another empowered by law and time-honored custom to prescribe the privileges to be enjoyed and the duties to be discharged by you; and then if you can imagine yourself to be content and happy, judge your mother and sisters and all women to be.

It was not because the three-penny tax on tea was so exorbitant that our Revolutionary fathers fought and died, but to establish the principle that such taxation was unjust. It is the same with this woman's revolution; though every law were as just to woman as to man, the principle that one class may usurp the power to legislate for another is unjust, and all who are now in the struggle from love of principle would still work on until the establishment of the grand and immutable truth, 'All governments derive their just powers from the consent of the governed!'

The Right to Strike

Sentence was passed on Saturday on the twenty 'men who had determined not to work.'

What was their offence?

They had said to one another, 'Let us come out of meanness and misery. Let us do what every order more privileged and more honored is doing every day. By the means which we believe to be the best let us raise ourselves and our families above the humbleness of our condition. We may be wrong, but we cannot help believing that we might do much if we were true brothers to each other, and would resolve not to sell the only thing which is our own, the cunning of our hands, for less than it is worth.'

They were condemned because they had determined not to work for the wages that were offered them! Can anything be imagined more abhorrent to every sentiment of generosity, of justice, than the law which arms the rich with the legal right to fix, by assize, the wages of the poor? If this is not SLAVERY, we have forgotten its definition. Strike the right of associating for the sale of labor from the privileges of a Freeman, and you may as well at once bind him to a master or ascribe him to the soil. If it be not in the color of his skin, and in the poor franchise of naming his own terms in a contract for his work, what advantage has the laborer of the North over the bondsmen of the South?

SUSAN B. ANTHONY
From a letter written to her brother, Daniel R. Anthony, in 1859.

WILLIAM CULLEN BRYANT
The Evening Post, New York, Monday, June 13, 1836.

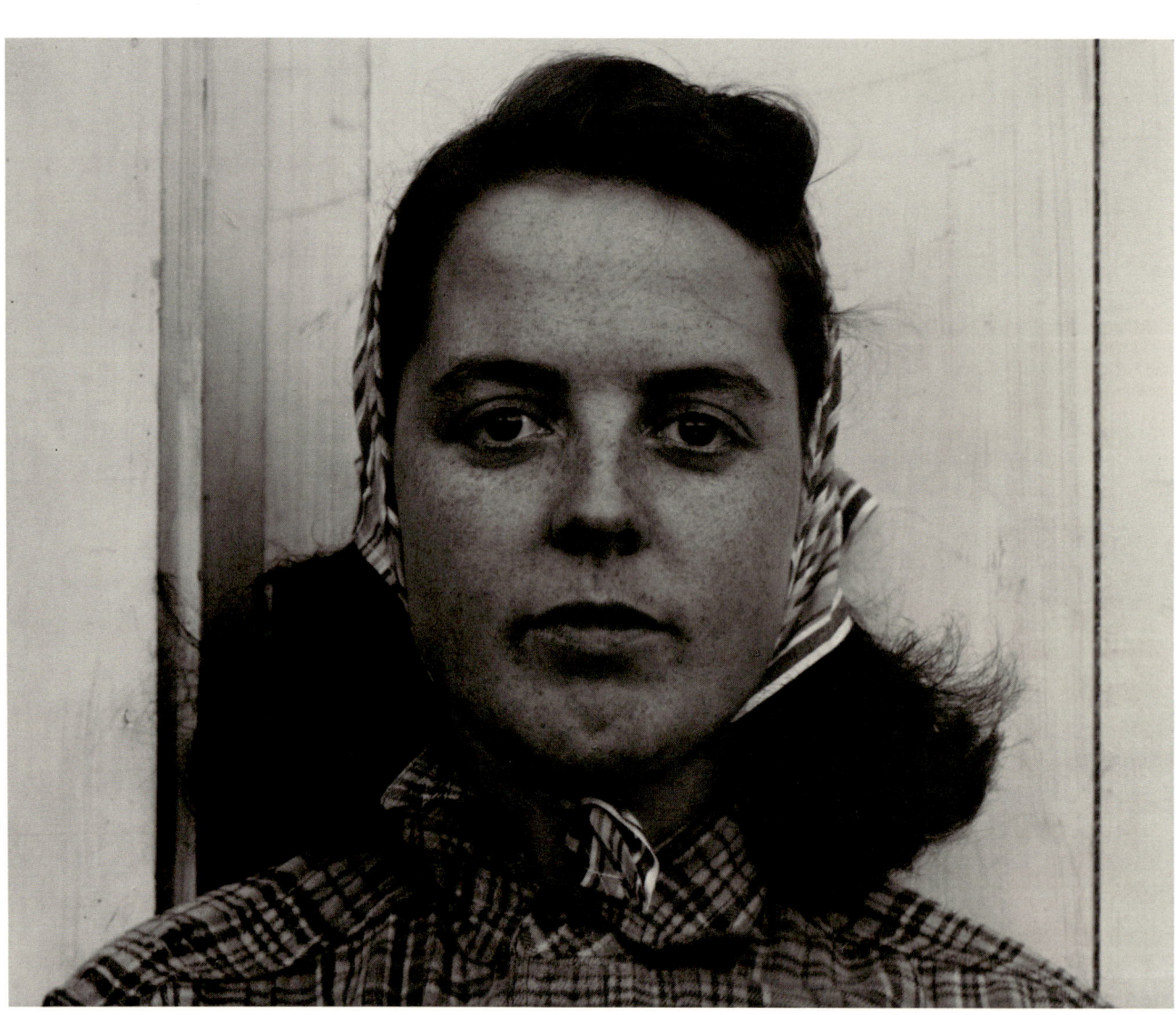

TURN-OUT, 1836

One of the first strikes of cotton-factory operatives that ever took place in this country was that in Lowell, in October 1836. When it was announced that the wages were to be cut down, great indignation was felt, and it was decided to strike, *en masse*. This was done. The mills were shut down, and the girls went in procession from the several corporations to the grove on Chapel Hill, and listened to 'incendiary speeches' from early labor reformers.

One of the girls stood on a pump, and gave vent to the feelings of her companions in a neat speech, declaring that it was their duty to resist all attempts at cutting down the wages. This was the first time a woman had spoken in public at Lowell, and the event caused surprise and consternation among her audience. It was estimated that as many as twelve or fifteen hundred girls turned out, and walked in procession through the streets. They had neither flags nor music, but sang songs.

My own recollection of this first strike (or 'turn out' as it was called) is very vivid. I worked in a lower room, where I had heard the proposed strike fully, if not vehemently, discussed; I had been an ardent listener and naturally I took sides with the strikers. When the day came on which the girls were to turn out, those in the upper rooms started first, and so many of them left that our mill was at once shut down. Then, when the girls in my room stood irresolute, uncertain what to do, asking each other, 'Would you?' or 'Shall we turn out?' and not one of them having the courage to lead off, I, who began to think they would not go out, after all their talk, became impatient, and started on ahead, saying with childish bravado, 'I don't care what you do, *I* am going to turn out, whether any one else does or not'; and I marched out, and was followed by the others.

The agent of the corporation where I then worked took some small revenges on the supposed ring-leaders; on the principle of sending the weaker to the wall, my mother was turned away from her boarding house, that functionary saying, 'Mrs Hanson, you could not prevent the older girls from turning out, but your daughter is a child, and *her* you could control.'

It is hardly necessary to say that so far as results were concerned this strike did no good. The dissatisfaction of the operatives subsided, or burned itself out, and though the authorities did not accede to their demands, the majority returned to their work, and the corporation went on cutting down wages.

HARRIET H. ROBINSON
Loom and Spindle, New York, 1898.

NEW ENGLAND AND THE LABOR MOVEMENT

My ideal of a civilization is a very high one; but the approach to it is a New England town of some two thousand inhabitants, with no rich man and no poor man in it, all mingling in the same society, every child at the same school, no poor house, no beggar, opportunities equal, nobody too proud to stand aloof, nobody too humble to be shut out. That's New England as it was fifty years ago.

The civilization that lingers beautifully on the hillsides of New England, nestles sweetly in the valleys of Vermont, the moment it approaches a crowd like Boston, or a million of men gathered in one place like New York,—rots.

But that isn't anything. You should go up to beautiful Berkshire with me, into the factories there. It shall be the day after a Presidential election. I will go with you into a counting-room,—four hundred employees. The partners are sitting down. They take the list of workmen, and sift them out; and every man that has not voted the ticket they wanted is thrown out to starve just as if he were cattle. That's Christian civilization! that's Massachusetts! I don't like that significant fact. I leap from that town into a large mill, with five hundred employees, and say to the master, 'How about the dwellings of your operatives? How many hours do they have at home?' 'Well, I hope they don't have any. The best-ventilated place they are ever in is my mill. They had better stay here sixteen hours out of the twenty-four; it keeps them out of mischief better than any other place. As long as they work, they are not doing worse. I cannot attend to their houses.' I say to him, 'It seems to me you do the same for your ox.' That's another significant fact of our civilization. I go to Lowell, and I say to a young girl, wandering in the street, 'How is this?' 'Well, I worked here seven years, and I thought I would leave that mill and go to another, and the corporation won't give me my ticket. I have sued them in the Supreme Court, and I cannot get it; and here I am, penniless, in Eastern Massachusetts.' That's Christian civilization. I am picking up, not individual facts, but significant rules that were made for labor. You say, 'What does labor need in New England?' It needs justice.

WENDELL PHILLIPS
'The Foundation of the Labor Movement,' 1871.

DEMOCRACY AND SOCIETY, 1840

I took in regard to society, even as late as 1840, the Democratic premises as true and unquestionable. They were given me by the public sentiment of my country. I had taken them in with my mother's milk, and had never thought of inquiring whether they were tenable or not. I took them as my political and social starting-point, or principium, and sought simply to harmonize government and society with them.

I contended that the great, the mother evil of modern society was the separation of capital and labor; or the fact that one class of the community owns the funds and another and a distinct class is compelled to perform the labor of production. The consequence of this system is, that owners of capital enrich themselves at the expense of the owners of labor. The system of money wages, the modern system, is more profitable to the owners of capital than the slave-system is to the slave-masters, and hardly less oppressive to the laborer.

The laborer sells his labor that he may not die of hunger, he, his wife, and little ones; and as the urgency of guarding against hunger is always stronger than that of growing rich or richer, the capitalist holds the laborer at his mercy, and has over him, whether called a slave or a freeman, the power of life and death. Dependent on wages alone, the laborer remains always poor. In what are called prosperous times he may, by working early and late, and with all his might, retain enough of the proceeds of his labor to save him from actual want; but in what are called 'hard times,' cases of actual suffering for want of the necessaries of life, nay, of actual starvation, even in our own country, are no rare occurrences.

The evil does not stop there.

Moral worth and intellectual superiority count for nothing. Men, to be of any account in their town or city, must be rich, at least appear to be rich. The slow gains of patient toil and honest industry no longer suffice. There is in all classes an impatience to be rich. The most daring and reckless speculations are resorted to, and when honest means fail, dishonest, nay, criminal, means are adopted. All are striving to be, or to appear, what they are not, to work their way up to a higher social stratum, and hence society becomes hollow, a sham, a lie.

The capitalist and the workman belong to different species, and have little personal intercourse. The agent or man of business pays the workman his wages, and there ends the responsibility of the employer. The laborer has no further claim on him, and he may want and starve, or sicken and die—it is his own affair, with which the employer has nothing to do The one class become proud, haughty, cold, supercilious, contemptuous, or at best superbly indifferent, looking upon their laborers as appendages of their steam-engines, their spinning-jennies or their power-looms; the other class become envious, discontented, resentful, hostile, laboring under a sense of injustice, and waiting only the opportunity to right themselves.

To remedy these evils, I proposed to abolish the distinction between capitalists and laborers, employer and employed, by having every man an owner of the funds as well as the labor of production. The business men of the country saw as clearly as I did whither my propositions tended, and took the alarm; and as the business interests, rather than the agricultural and mechanical interests, ruled the minds of my countrymen, I had my labor for my pains. Here was the gravamen of my offence: I had dared take Democracy at its word, and push its principles to their last logical consequences; I had had the incredible folly of treating the equality asserted as if it meant something, as if it could be made a reality, instead of a miserable sham.

ORESTES BROWNSON
The Convert, or Leaves from My Experience, New York, 1857.

The March of Human Freedom

It is not for men long to hinder the march of human freedom.

You may gather all the dried grass and all the straw in both continents; you may braid it into ropes to bind down the sea; while it is calm you may laugh, and say, 'Lo, I have chained the ocean!' But when the winds blow their trumpets, the sea rises in its strength, snaps asunder the bonds that had confined his mighty limbs, and the world is littered with the idle hay!

Stop the human race in its development and march to freedom? As well might the boys of Boston, some lustrous night, mounting the steeples of this town, call on the stars to stay their course! Gently, but irresistibly, the Greater and the Lesser Bear move round the pole; Orion in his mighty mail comes up the sky; the Bull, the Ram, the Heavenly Twins, the Crab, the Lion, the Maid, the Scales, and all that shining company, pursue their march all night, and the new day discovers the idle urchins in their lofty places, all tired, and sleepy, and ashamed.

Do you know how empires find their end? Yes, the great states eat up the little. As with fish, so with nations. Aye, but how do the great states come to an end? By their own injustice, and no other cause.

THEODORE PARKER
The State of the Nation, Thanksgiving Day sermon, Boston, November 28, 1850.

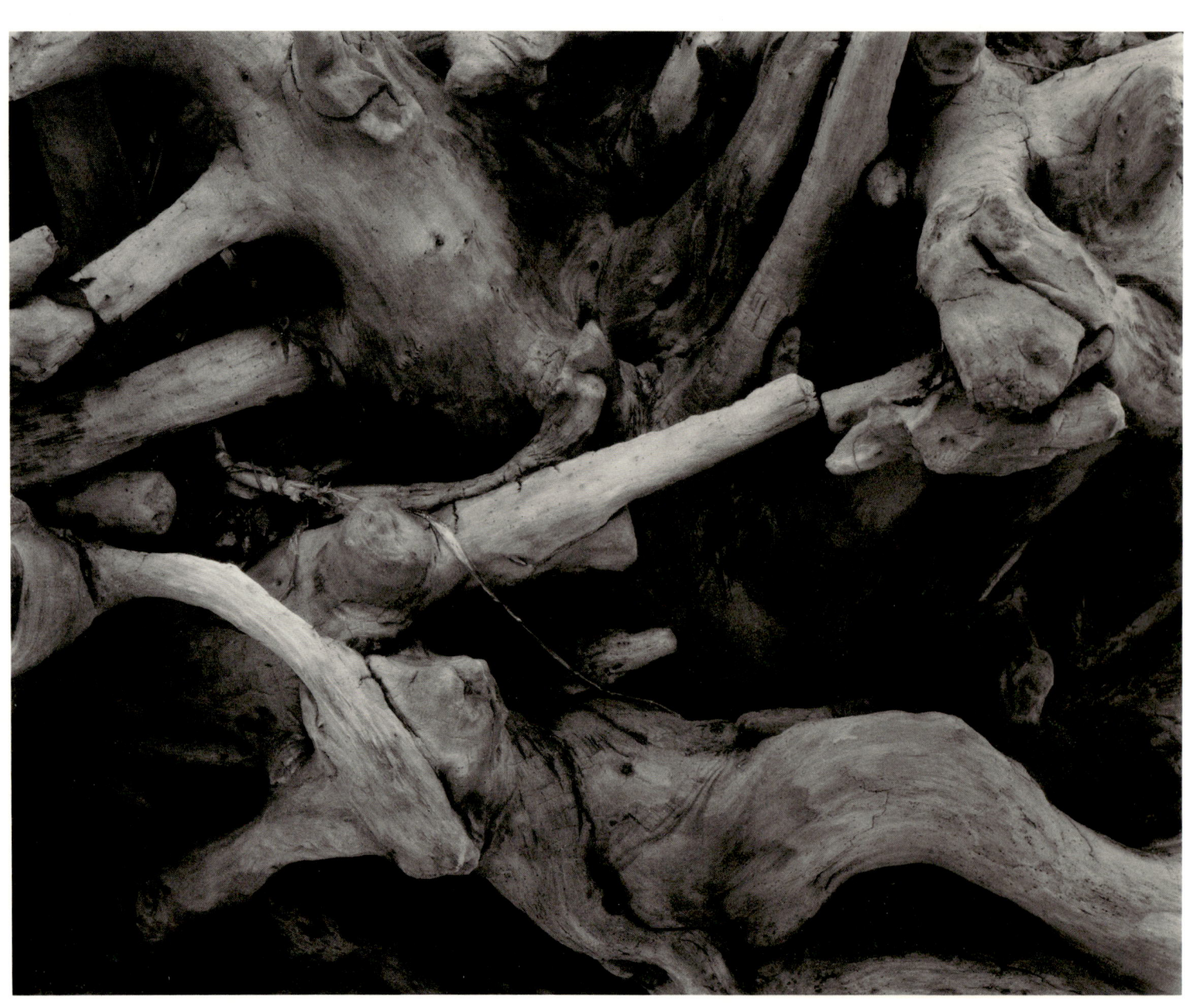

5 *Abolition*

Cayenne, April 23, 1789

Honor'd Parent:
We sailed from Cape Mount the 13th March with 36 slaves on board. The 26th day of March the slaves rised upon us. At half-past seven, my Sire and hands being forward except the man at the helm, and myself, three of the slaves took possession of the cabin and two upon the quarterdeck. Them in the cabin took possession of the firearms, and them on the quarter-deck with the axe and cutlash and other weapons. Them in the cabin handed up pistols to them on the quarter-deck.

One of them fired and killed my honored Sire, and then we got on the quarter-deck and killed two of them. One that was in the cabin was coming out at the cabin windows in order to get on deck, and we discovered him and knocked him overboard.

Then three men went forward and got the three that was down there and brought them aft. We put them in irons and chained them and then the doctor dressed the people's wounds. Then it was one o'clock.

They buried my Honored Parent, he was buried as decent as he could be at sea. I scalt myself with hot chocolate but now I am able to walk about again. So I remain in good health and hope to find you the same and all my brothers and sisters and all that inquires after me. We have sold part of the slaves and I hope to be home soon.

So I remain your dutiful son,
Wm Fairfield

WILLIAM FAIRFIELD
Addressed to Mrs. Rebecca Fairfield, Salem, New England.

LETTER TO THE HONORABLE CHARLES SUMNER

Entering a large paved courtyard, around which ran galleries filled with slaves of all ages, sexes, and colors, I heard the snap of a whip, every stroke of which sounded like the sharp crack of a pistol. I turned my head and beheld a sight which absolutely chilled me to the marrow of my bones, and gave me for the first time in my life, the sensation of my hair stiffening at the roots.

There lay a black girl flat upon her face, on a board, her two thumbs tied and fastened to one end, her feet tied and drawn tightly to the other end, while a strap passed over the small of her back, and, fastened around the board, compressed her tightly to it. Below the strap she was entirely naked. By her side, and six feet off, stood a huge Negro, with a long whip, which he applied with dreadful power and wonderful precision. Every stroke brought away a strip of skin, which clung to the lash, or fell quivering on the pavement, while the blood followed after it. The poor creature writhed and shrieked, and, in a voice which showed alike her fear of death and her dreadful agony, screamed to her master, who stood at her head, 'O, spare my life! don't cut my soul out!' But still fell the horrid lash; still strip after strip peeled off from the skin; gash after gash was cut in her living flesh, until it became a livid and bleeding mass of raw and quivering muscle. It was with the greatest difficulty I refrained from springing upon the torturer, and arresting his lash; but, alas! what could I do, but turn aside to hide my tears for the sufferer? This was in a public and regularly-organized prison; the punishment was one recognized and authorized by the law. But think you the poor wretch had committed a heinous offence, and had been convicted thereof, and sentenced to the lash? Not at all. She was brought by her master to be whipped by the common executioner, without trial, judge or jury, just at his beck or nod, for some real or supposed offence, or to gratify his own whim or malice. And he may bring her day after day, without cause assigned, and inflict any number of lashes he pleases, short of twenty-five, provided only he pays the fee.

DR. SAMUEL GRIDLEY HOWE
Quoted by Harriet Beecher Stowe in *A Key to Uncle Tom's Cabin*, London, 1853.

To John Taylor, to Eschew Politics and Speed the Plough

Washington, 17 March, 1852

John Taylor,—
Go ahead. The heart of the winter is broken, and before the first day of April all your land may be ploughed. Put the great oxen in a condition to be turned out to be fattened. I know not when I shall see you, but I hope before planting. Whatever ground you sow or plant, see that it is in good condition. We want no pennyroyal crops.

'A little farm well tilled,'

is to a farmer the next best thing to

'A little wife well-willed.'

Cultivate your garden. I have sent you many garden seeds. Distribute them among your neighbors; send them to the stores in the village, that everybody may have a part of them without cost.

I am glad that you have chosen Mr Pike representative. He is a true man; but there are in New Hampshire many persons, who call themselves Whigs, who are no Whigs at all, and no better than disunionists. Any man, who hesitates in granting and securing to every part of the country its just and constitutional rights, is an enemy to the whole country. John Taylor! if one of your boys should say that he honors his father and mother, and loves his brothers and sisters, but still insists that one of them shall be driven out of the family, what can you say of him but that there is no real family love in him? You and I are farmers, we never talk politics; our talk is of oxen; but remember this: that any man who attempts to excite one part of this country against another, is just as wicked as he would be who should attempt to get up a quarrel between John Taylor and his neighbor old Mr John Sanborn, or his other neighbor Captain Burleigh. There are some animals that live best in the fire; and there are some men, who delight in heat, smoke, combustion, and even general conflagration. They do not follow the things which make for peace. Have no communion with such persons, either as neighbors or politicians. You have no more right to say that slavery ought not to exist in Virginia, than a Virginian has to say that slavery ought to exist in New Hampshire. This is a question left to every State to decide for itself, and if we mean to keep the States together, we must leave to every State this power of deciding for itself.

I think I never wrote you a word before upon politics. I shall not do it again. I only say love your country and your whole country.

John Taylor! you are a free man; you possess good principles, you have a large family to rear and provide for by your labor. Be thankful to the government, which does not oppress you, which does not bear you down by excessive taxation; but which holds out to you and yours the hope of all the blessings which liberty, industry, and security give.

John Taylor! thank God, morning and evening, that you were born in such a country. John Taylor! never write me another word upon politics.

Give my kindest remembrance to your wife and children; and when you look from your eastern windows upon the graves of my family, remember that he, who is the author of this letter, must soon follow them to another world.

DANIEL WEBSTER

To the Public

During my recent tour for the purpose of exciting the minds of the people on the subject of slavery, every place that I visited gave fresh evidence of the fact, that a greater revolution in public sentiment was to be effected in the Free States—*and particularly in New England*—than in the South. I found contempt more bitter, opposition more active, detraction more relentless, prejudice more stubborn, and apathy more frozen than among the slave-owners themselves. I determined, at every hazard, to lift up the standard of emancipation in the eye of the nation, *within sight of Bunker Hill and in the birthplace of liberty*.

I am aware that many object to the severity of my language; but is there not cause for severity. I *will be* as harsh as truth, and as uncompromising as justice. On this subject, I do not wish to think, or speak, or write, with moderation. No! no! Tell a man whose house in on fire to give a moderate alarm; tell him to moderately rescue his wife from the hands of the ravisher; tell the mother to gradually rescue her baby from the fire into which it has fallen;—but urge me not to use moderation in a cause like the present. I am in earnest—I will not equivocate—I will not excuse—I will not retreat a single inch—and I will be heard.

WILLIAM LLOYD GARRISON
Manifesto in the first number of *The Liberator*, 1831.

Meeting of the Boston Female Anti-Slavery Society

Broken up by a Mob of 'Gentlemen of Property and Standing,' 21 October, 1835

James L. Homer, editor, Commercial Gazette:

There was much feeling, and much indignation expressed in private, among business men, in relation to the proposed meeting—the *men* thinking that *women* ought to be at home, attending to their domestic arrangements, instead of sowing the seeds of political discord at the Anti-Slavery rooms.

On the morning of the meeting, I was waited upon by 'a committee of two'—both merchants on Central Wharf—who requested me to write, print, and cause to be distributed an inflammatory handbill in relation to the meeting—'something that would wake up the populace'—and they would pay the expense. I complied, most cheerfully:

THOMPSON
THE ABOLITIONIST!!!

That infamous foreign scoundrel, Thompson, will hold forth *this afternoon* at the Liberator office, No. 48 Washington Street. The present is a fair opportunity for the friends of the Union to *snake Thompson out!* A purse of $100 has been raised by a number of patriotic citizens to reward the individual who shall first lay violent hands on Thompson, so that he may be brought to the tar-kettle before dark. Friends of the Union, be vigilant!

Boston, Wednesday, 12 o'clock

Mrs Maria Weston Chapman, member of the Boston Female Anti-Slavery Society:

The tumult continually increased, with horrible execrations, howling, stamping, and finally shrieking with rage. A row of hostile heads appeared over the slight partition, of half the height of the wall, which divides the Society's room from the landing place.

William Lloyd Garrison, editor of the Liberator:

In the meantime, the crowd in the street had augmented from a hundred to thousands. The cry was for 'Thompson! Thompson!'—but the Mayor had now arrived, and, addressing the rioters, he assured them that Mr Thompson was not in the city, and besought them to disperse.

Mrs Chapman:

The slight partition began to yield. The mob hurled missiles at the lady presiding. The secretary rose and began to read her report, utterly inaudible from the confusion. At this moment Mr Lyman entered.

Mr Lyman. I am the mayor of this town. Ladies, do you wish to see a scene of bloodshed and confusion? If you do not, go home.

One of the Ladies. Mr Lyman, your personal friends are the instigators of this mob; have you ever used your personal influence with them?

Mr Lyman. I know no personal friends; I am merely an official. Indeed, ladies, you must retire. It is dangerous to remain.

Lady. If this is the last bulwark of freedom, we may as well die here as anywhere.

Mr Lyman. You cannot die here.

When we emerged into the open daylight, there went up a roar of rage and contempt, which increased when they saw that we did not intend to separate, but walked in regular procession, two and two, each with a colored friend. They slowly gave way as we came out. As far as we could look either way, the crowd extended—evidently of the so-called 'wealthy and respectable'; 'the moral worth'; 'the influence and standing.' We saw the faces of those we had, till now, thought friends; men whom we had never before met without giving the hand in friendly salutation.

Garrison:

'*Garrison* is there!' was the cry. 'Garrison! Garrison! We must have Garrison! Out with him! Lynch him!'

A this juncture an abolition brother, in his anguish and alarm for my safety, said—'I must henceforth repudiate the principle of non-resistance. When the civil arm is powerless, my own rights are trodden in the dust, and the lives of my friends are put in imminent peril by ruffians.' Putting my hand on his shoulder, I said, 'This is the trial of our faith and the test of our endurance. Do you wish to become like one of these violent and bloodthirsty men who are seeking my life? God forbid! I will perish sooner than raise my hand against any man, even in self-defence, and let none of my friends resort to violence for my protection. If my life be taken, the cause of emancipation will not suffer.'

I dropped from a backwindow, and narrowly escaped falling headlong. We entered a carpenter's shop, through which we attempted to get into Wilson's Lane, but found our retreat cut off by the mob. They raised a shout as soon as we came in sight, but the workmen closed the door of the shop, kept them at bay for a time. In a few minutes several ruffians broke into the chamber. On seeing me three or four uttering a yell, furiously dragged me to the window, with the intention of hurling me from that height to the ground, but one of them relented and said—'Don't let us kill him outright.'

Spinal Vance, son of a grain merchant:

I had thought it was good sport up to this time, but when I saw him standing there so pale I thought it was going too far, and said to Aaron Cooley, Let's go to the rescue; and with some more who helped us we got him clear.

Charles Sprague, banker and poet:

I saw an exasperated mob dragging a man along without his hat and with a rope about him. The man walked with head erect, calm countenance, flashing eyes, like a martyr going to the stake.

Garrison:

They led me along bareheaded through a mighty crowd, ever and anon shouting, 'He shan't be hurt. Don't hurt him! He is an American,' &c., &c. I was thus conducted over the ground that was stained with the blood of the first martyrs in the cause of Liberty and Independence, by the memorable massacre of 1770. And upon that 'consecrated spot,' I was made an object of derision and scorn, and my body was denuded of a large portion of its covering.

The Mayor and his advisers came to the singular conclusion that the preservation of my life depended upon committing me to jail, ostensibly as a disturber of the peace! A hack was got in readiness. The mob, enraged by a series of disappointments, did rush like a whirlwind upon the frail vehicle in which I sat, and did endeavor to drag me out of it. They clung to the wheels—dashed open the doors—seized hold of the horse—and tried to upset the carriage. They were, however, vigorously repulsed by the police—a constable sprang in by my side— the doors were closed—and the driver, lustily using his whip upon the bodies of his horses and the heads of the rioters, made an opening through the crowd, and drove at a tremendous speed. But many of the rioters followed and repeatedly attempted to arrest the horses. We drove up to the new and last refuge of liberty and life, another bold attempt was made to seize me by the mob,—but in vain. In a few minutes I was locked up in a cell, safe from my persecutors, accompanied by a good conscience and a cheerful mind.

Excerpts from *William Lloyd Garrison, The Story of His Life Told by His Children,* Boston and New York, 1894.

THE MURDER OF LOVEJOY

NOTE: In November 1837, a mob in Alton, Illinois, shot and killed the Rev. E. P. Lovejoy, abolitionist editor, while he was trying to defend his presses. This murder split the nation into violently opposing factions. At a mass meeting at Faneuil Hall, Boston, the Hon. James T. Austin, Attorney General for Massachusetts, attacked the abolitionists, called Lovejoy presumptuous and the slaves a menagerie, and compared the Alton mob to the Boston Tea Party. He was at once wildly applauded and vehemently booed. In the commotion, young Wendell Phillips, who had never spoken in public before and had not expected to say anything, finally succeeded in gaining the floor.

Fellow citizens, is this Faneuil Hall doctrine?

NO, NO!

The mob at Alton were met to wrest from a citizen his just rights,—met to resist the laws. We have been told that our fathers did the same; and the glorious mantle of Revolutionary precedent has been thrown over the mobs of our day. Sir, when I heard the gentleman lay down principles which place the murderers of Alton side by side with Otis and Hancock, with Quincy and Adams, I thought those pictured lips *(pointing to the portraits on the walls)* would have broken into voice to rebuke the recreant American,—the slanderer of the dead.

GREAT APPLAUSE AND COUNTERAPPLAUSE.

The gentleman said that he should sink into insignificance if he dared to gainsay the principles of these resolutions. Sir, for the sentiments he had uttered, on soil consecrated by the prayers of Puritans and the blood of Patriots, the earth should have yawned and swallowed him up.

UPROAR. APPLAUSE, HISSES, CRIES OF 'TAKE THAT BACK' FINALLY QUIETED BY APPEALS FOR FREE DISCUSSION.

Presumptuous to assert the freedom of the press on American ground? Who invents this libel on his country? It is this very thing which entitles Lovejoy to greater praise. The disputed right which provoked the Revolution—taxation without representation—is far beneath that for which he died.

STRONG AND GENERAL DISAPPROVAL.

One word, gentlemen. As much as thought is better than money, so much is the cause in which Lovejoy died nobler than a mere question of taxes. James Otis thundered in this Hall when the King did but touch his *pocket*. Imagine, if you can, his indignant eloquence, had England offered to put a gag upon his lips.

GREAT APPLAUSE.

Mr Chairman, from the bottom of my heart I thank that brave little band in Alton for resisting. We must remember that Lovejoy had fled from city to city,—suffered the destruction of three presses patiently. It was full time to assert the laws. The people there, children of our older states, seem to have forgotten the blood-tried principles of their fathers the moment they lost sight of our New England hills. Something was to be done to show them the priceless value of the freedom of the press, to bring back and set right their wandering and confused ideas. He and his advisers looked out on a community staggering like a drunken man. Deaf to argument, haply they might be stunned into sobriety. Insulted law called for it. Public opinion, fast hastening on the downward course, must be arrested.

Does not the event show they judged rightly? Men begin, as in 1776 and 1640, to discuss principles, to weigh characters, to find out where they are. Haply we may awake before we are borne over the precipice.

WENDELL PHILLIPS
Speeches, Lectures, and Letters, Boston, 1863.

Abolition

May, 1851

I have had to arm myself. I have written my sermons with a pistol in my desk,—loaded, a cap on the nipple, and ready for action. Yea, with a drawn sword within reach of my right hand. This I have done in Boston; in the midst of the nineteenth century; been obliged to do it to defend the [innocent] members of my church, women as well as men. You know that I do not like fighting.

But what could I do? I was born in the little town where the first bloodshed of the Revolution began. The bones of men who first fell in that war are covered by the monument at Lexington, it is 'sacred to Liberty and the Rights of Mankind.' Those men fell 'in the sacred cause of God and their country.' This is the first inscription I ever read. These men were my kindred. My grandfather drew the first sword in the Revolution; my fathers fired the first shot; the blood which flowed there was kindred to this which courses in my veins today.

Besides that, when I write in my library at home, on the one side of me is the Bible which my fathers prayed over, their morning and evening prayer, for nearly a hundred years. On the other side there hangs the firelock my grandfather fought with in the old French war, which he carried at the taking of Quebec, which he zealously used at the battle of Lexington, and beside it is another, a trophy of that war, the first gun taken in the Revolution, taken also by my grandfather.

With these things before me, these symbols; with these memories in me, when a parishioner, a fugitive from slavery, a woman, pursued by the kidnappers, came to my house, what could I do less than take her in and defend her to the last?

The Rescue of Shadrach, Arrested Under the Fugitive Slave Law

February, 1851

On the day of the arraignment of the supposed fugitive, the fact was noted in a newspaper by a colored man of great energy and character, employed by a firm in Boston, and utterly unconnected with the Abolitionists. He asked leave of absence, and strolled into the Court-House. Many colored men were at the door and had been excluded; but he being known and trusted, was admitted, and the others, making a rush, followed in behind him with a hubbub of joking and laughter. There were but a few constables on duty, and it suddenly struck this leader, as he and his followers passed near, that they might as well keep on and pass out at the opposite door, taking with them the man under arrest, who was not handcuffed. After a moment's beckoning, the prisoner saw his opportunity, fell in with the jubilant procession, and amid continued uproar was got outside the Court-House, when the crowd scattered in all directions.

THE REVEREND THEODORE PARKER
Additional Speeches and Occasional Sermons, vol. 1, Boston, 1855.

COLONEL THOMAS WENTWORTH HIGGINSON
Cheerful Yesterdays, Boston, 1901.

*Plot to Rescue Anthony Burns, Arrested under
the Fugitive Slave Law, May 7, 1854*

The effort must have behind it the momentum of a public meeting, such as was to be held at Faneuil Hall that night. Could there not be an attack at the very height of the meeting, brought about in this way? Let all be in readiness; let a picked body be distributed near the Court-House and Square; then send some loud-voiced speaker, who should appear in the gallery of Faneuil Hall and announce that there was a mob of Negroes already attacking the Court-House; let a speaker, previously warned,—Phillips, if possible—accept the opportunity promptly, and send the whole meeting pell mell to Court Square, ready to fall in behind the leaders and bring out the slave. I accepted it heartily, and think now, as I thought then, that it was one of the very best plots that ever—failed.

It was the largest gathering I ever saw in that hall. The platform was covered with men; the galleries, the floor, even the outer stairways, were absolutely filled with a solid audience. When the speaking was once begun, we could no more communicate with the platform than if the Atlantic Ocean rolled between.

Those of us who had been told off to be ready in Court Square went there singly, not to attract attention. No sign of motion or life was there, though the lights gleamed from many windows. Planting myself near a door which stood ajar, I waited. The moments seemed endless. Presently a rush of running figures, like the sweep of a wave, came round the corner of Court Square. The crowd ran on pell mell, and I scanned it for a familiar face. A single glance brought the conviction of failure and disappointment. We had the froth and scum of the meeting, the fringe of idlers on its edge. The men on the platform, the real nucleus of that great gathering, were far in the rear, perhaps were still clogged in the hall. An official ran up from the basement, looked me in the face, ran in, and locked the door.

Mingling with the crowd, I ran against Stowell. He whispered, 'Some of our men are bringing a beam up to the west door.' Instantly he and I ran round and grasped the beam, I finding myself at the head, with a stout Negro opposite me.

Taking the joist up the steps, we hammered away at the southwest door. It could not have been many minutes before it began to give way, was then secured again, then swung ajar, and rested heavily, one hinge having parted. There was room for but one to pass in. I glanced instinctively at my black ally. He did not even look at me, but sprang in first, I following. In later years the experience was of inestimable value to me, for it removed once for all every doubt of the intrinsic courage of the blacks. We found ourselves inside, face to face with six or eight policemen, who laid about them with their clubs, driving us to the wall and hammering away at our heads. Often as I had heard of clubbing, I had never known just how it felt, and to my surprise it was not half so bad as I expected. I did not know that I received a severe cut on the chin, whose scar I yet carry, though still ignorant how it came. Nor did I know till next morning, what had a more important bearing on the seeming backwardness of my supposed comrades, that, just as the door sprang open, a shot had been fired, and one of the marshal's deputies, a man named Batchelder, had fallen dead. There had been other fugitive slave rescues in different parts of the country, but this was the first drop of blood actually shed.

We were gradually forced back beyond the threshold, the door standing now wide open, and our supporters hav-

Abolition

ing fallen back to leave the steps free. Not knowing that a man had already been killed, and that Stowell and others had just been taken off by the police, I held my place outside, still hoping against hope that some concerted reinforcements might appear. Meanwhile the deputy marshals retreated to the stairway, over which we could see their pistols pointing, the whole hall between us and them being brightly lighted.

In the silent pause that ensued there came quietly forth from the crowd the well-known form of Mr Amos Bronson Alcott, the Transcendental philosopher. Ascending the lighted steps alone, he said tranquilly, turning to me and pointing forward, 'Why are we not within?' 'Because,' was the rather impatient answer, 'these people will not stand by us.' He said not a word, but calmly walked up the steps,—he and his familiar cane. He paused again at the top, the centre of all eyes, within and without; a revolver sounded from within, but hit nobody; and finding himself wholly unsupported, he turned and retreated, but without hastening a step.

Years later the successor of the U. S. marshal said to me that his predecessor had told him that the surprise was complete, and that thirty resolute men could have carried off Burns. Had the private entrance to the platform in Faneuil Hall existed then, as now, those thirty would certainly have been at hand.

The attempt being a failure, and troops approaching, I went down the steps. A man in the crowd sidled quietly up to me and placidly remarked, 'Mister, I guess you've left your rumberill.' It flashed through my mind that before taking hold of the beam I had set down my umbrella—for it was a showery day—over the railing of the Court-House steps. Recapturing this important bit of evidence, I made my way to Dr W. F. Channing's house, had my cut attended to, and went to bed.

COLONEL THOMAS WENTWORTH HIGGINSON
Cheerful Yesterdays, Boston, 1901.

JOHN BROWN'S HOUSEHOLD, 1859

The notch seems beyond the world, North Elba and its half dozen houses are beyond the Notch, and there is a wilder little mountain road which rises beyond North Elba. But the house we seek is not even on that road, but behind it and beyond it; you ride a mile or two, then take down a pair of bars; beyond the bars, faith takes you across a half-cleared field, through the most difficult of wood-paths, and after half a mile of forest you come out upon a clearing. There is a little frame house, unpainted, set in a girdle of black stumps, and with all heaven about it for a wider girdle; on a high hill-side, forests on north and west,—the glorious line of the Adirondacks on the east, and on the south one slender road leading off to Westport,—a road so straight that you could sight a United States marshal for five miles.

There stands the little house with no ornament or relief about it—it needs none with the setting of mountain horizon. Yes, there is one decoration which, stern and misplaced as it would seem elsewhere, seems appropriate here . . . an old, mossy, time-worn tombstone,—not marking any grave, not set in the ground, but resting against the house as if its time were either past or not yet come. Both are true—it has a past duty and a future one. It bears the name of Captain John Brown, who died during the Revolution, eighty-three years ago; it was brought hither by his grandson bearing the same name and title; the latter caused to be inscribed upon it, also, the name of his son Frederick, 'murdered at Osawatomie for his adherence to the cause of freedom' (so reads the inscription); and he himself has said that no other tombstone should mark his own grave. As the two lately wedded sons went forth joyfully on their father's call to keep their last pledge at Harper's Ferry, they issued from that doorway between their weeping wives on the one side and that ancestral stone on the other. 'They could not,' they told their mother and their wives, 'live for themselves alone,' and so they went.

It had been my privilege to live in the best society all my life—namely, that of abolitionists and fugitive slaves. I had seen the most eminent persons of the age: several men on whose heads tens of thousands of dollars had been set; a black woman [Harriet Tubman], who, after escaping from slavery herself, had gone back secretly eight times into the jaws of death to bring out persons she had never seen; and a white man, who, after assisting away fugitives by the thousand, had twice been stripped of every dollar of his property in fines, and, when taunted by the court, had mildly said, 'Friend, if thee knows any poor fugitive in need of breakfast, send him to Thomas Garrett's door.' I had known these, and such as these; but I had not known the Browns.

Here was a family out of which four young men had within a fortnight been killed. I say nothing of a father under a sentence of death, and a brother fleeing for his life, but only speak of those killed. As I sat that evening, with the women busily sewing around me, preparing the mother for her sudden departure with me on the morrow, some daguerreotypes were brought out to show me, and some one said, 'This is Oliver, one of those who were killed at Harper's Ferry.' I glanced up sidelong at the young, fair-haired girl, who sat near me by the little table—a wife at fifteen, a widow at sixteen; and this was her husband, and he was killed. As the words were spoken in her hearing, not a muscle quivered, and her fingers did not tremble as she drew the thread. Her life had become too real to leave room for wincing at mere words. She had lived through, beyond the word, to the sterner fact, and having confronted that, language was an empty shell. To the Browns, killing means simply dying—nothing more; one gate into heaven, and that one a good deal frequented by their family; that is all.

Their mother spoke the spirit of them all to me, next day, when she said, 'I have had thirteen children, and only four are left; but if I am to see the ruin of my house, I cannot hope that Providence may bring out of it some benefit to the poor slaves.'

'Her husband always believed,' she said, 'that he was to be an instrument in the hands of Providence,' and she believed it too. 'This plan had occupied his thought and prayers for twenty years.' 'Many a night he had lain awake, and prayed concerning it.' 'For herself,' she said, 'she had always prayed that her husband might be killed in fight rather than fall alive into the hands of slaveholders, but she could not regret it now, in view of the noble words of freedom which it had been his privilege to utter.' The next day, on the railway, I was compelled to put into her hands the newspaper containing the death warrant of her husband. She read it, and then the tall, strong woman bent her head for a few minutes on the back of the seat before us; then she raised it, and spoke calmly as before.

COLONEL THOMAS WENTWORTH HIGGINSON
Contemporaries, Boston, 1899.

A Plea for Captain John Brown

I am here to plead his cause with you. I plead not for his life, but for his character,—his immortal life; and so it becomes your cause wholly; and is not his in the least. Some eighteen hundred years ago Christ was crucified; this morning perchance, Captain Brown was hung. These are the two ends of a chain which is not without its links. He is not Old Brown any longer; he is an angel of light.

I see now that it was necessary that the bravest and humanest man in all the country should be hung. Perhaps he saw it himself. I *almost fear* that I may yet hear of his deliverance, doubting if a prolonged life, if *any* life, can do as much good as his death.

'Misguided!' 'Garrulous!' 'Insane!' 'Vindictive!' So ye write in your easy-chairs, and thus he wounded responds from the floor of the Armory, clear as a cloudless sky, true as the voice of nature is: 'No man sent me here; it was my own prompting and that of my Maker. I acknowledge no master in human form.'

And in what a sweet and noble strain he proceeds, addressing his captors, who stand over him: 'I think, my friends, you are guilty of a great wrong against God and humanity, and it would be perfectly right for anyone to interfere with you so far as to free those you willfully and wickedly hold in bondage.'

And, referring to his movement: 'It is, in my opinion, the greatest service a man can render to God.'

'I pity the poor in bondage that have none to help them; that is why I am here; not to gratify any personal animosity, revenge, or vindictive spirit. It is my sympathy with the oppressed and the wronged, that are as good as you, and as precious in the sight of God.'

You don't know your testament when you see it.

'I want you to understand that I respect the rights of the poorest and weakest of colored people, oppressed by the slave power, just as much as I do those of the most wealthy and powerful.'

'I wish to say, furthermore, that you had better, all of you people at the South, prepare yourselves for a settlement of that question, that must come up for settlement sooner than you are prepared for it. The sooner you are prepared the better. You may dispose of me very easily. I am nearly disposed of now; but this question is still to be settled,—this Negro question, I mean; the end of that is not yet.'

I foresee the time when the painter will paint that scene, no longer going to Rome for a subject; the poet will sing it; and, with the Landing of the Pilgrims and the Declaration of Independence, it will be the ornament of some future national gallery, when at least the present form of slavery shall be no more here. We shall then be at liberty to weep for Captain Brown. Then, and not till then, we will take our revenge.

HENRY DAVID THOREAU
From *A Yankee in Canada with Anti-Slavery and Reform Papers*
as quoted from an address delivered in Concord, October 30, 1859,
at a meeting summoned by Thoreau while Brown was still in prison.

PART FOUR

I *Ebb*

It is the age of severance, of disassociation, of freedom, of analysis, of detachment.

The new race is stiff, heady, and rebellious; they are fanatics in freedom, they hate tolls, taxes, turnpikes, banks, hierarchies, governors, yea, almost laws. They have a neck of unspeakable tenderness; it winces at a hair. They rebel against theological as against political dogmas; against meditation, or saints, or any nobility in the unseen.

The age of arithmetic and of criticism has set in.

In the law courts, crimes of fraud have taken the place of crimes of force. The stockbroker has taken the place of the war-like baron. The nobles shall not any longer, as feudal lords, have power of life and death over the churls, but now, in another shape, as capitalists, shall in all love and peace eat them up as before.

Instead of the social existence which all shared, was now separation. Everyone for himself; driven to find all his resources, hopes, rewards, society and deity within himself. The young men were born with knives in their brains, a tendency to introversion, self-dissection, anatomizing of motives.

RALPH WALDO EMERSON
'Historic Notes of Life and Letters in New England,'
Atlantic Monthly, October, 1883.

I *Ebb*

It is the age of severance, of disassociation, of freedom, of analysis, of detachment.

The new race is stiff, heady, and rebellious; they are fanatics in freedom, they hate tolls, taxes, turnpikes, banks, hierarchies, governors, yea, almost laws. They have a neck of unspeakable tenderness; it winces at a hair. They rebel against theological as against political dogmas; against meditation, or saints, or any nobility in the unseen.

The age of arithmetic and of criticism has set in.

In the law courts, crimes of fraud have taken the place of crimes of force. The stockbroker has taken the place of the war-like baron. The nobles shall not any longer, as feudal lords, have power of life and death over the churls, but now, in another shape, as capitalists, shall in all love and peace eat them up as before.

Instead of the social existence which all shared, was now separation. Everyone for himself; driven to find all his resources, hopes, rewards, society and deity within himself. The young men were born with knives in their brains, a tendency to introversion, self-dissection, anatomizing of motives.

RALPH WALDO EMERSON
'Historic Notes of Life and Letters in New England,'
Atlantic Monthly, October, 1883.

RETURN, 1868

At ten o'clock of a July night, in heat that made the tropical rain-shower shimmer, the Adams family* clambered down the side of their Cunard steamer into the government tugboat, which set them ashore in black darkness at the end of some North River pier. Had they been Tyrian traders of the year B.C. 1000, landing from a galley fresh from Gibraltar, they could hardly have been stranger on the shore of a world, so changed from what it had been ten years before.

One could divine pretty nearly where the force lay, since the last ten years had given the great mechanical energies—coal, iron, steam—a distinct superiority in power over the old industrial elements—agriculture, handwork, and learning; but the result of this revolution on a survivor from the fifties resembled the action of the earthworm; he twisted about, in vain, to recover his starting-point; he could no longer see his own trail; he had become an estray; a flotsam or jetsam of wreckage. His world was dead. He made no complaint and found no fault with his time; he was no worse off than the Indians or the buffalo who had been ejected from their heritage by his own people; but he vehemently insisted that he was not himself at fault. The defeat was not due to him, nor yet to any superiority in his rivals. He had been unfairly forced out of the track, and must get back into it as best he could.

The new Americans, of whom he was to be one, must, whether they were fit or unfit, create a world of their own, a science, a society, a philosophy, a universe, where they had not yet created a road, or even learned to dig their own iron. They had no time for thought; they saw, and could see, nothing beyond their day's work. Above all, they naturally disliked to be told what to do, and how to do it, by men who took their ideas and their methods from the abtract theories of history, philosophy, or theology. They knew enough to know that their world was one of energies quite new.

*During the Civil War, Charles Francis Adams, Senior, was United States Minister to England. His son Henry served as his private secretary.

HENRY ADAMS
The Education of Henry Adams, Boston, 1918.

BOSTON AND QUINCY

I may say that in the course of my life I have tried Boston socially on all sides; I have summered it and wintered it, tried it drunk and tried it sober; and, drunk or sober, there's nothing in it—save Boston!

This is the trouble with Boston—it is provincial. Including Cambridge, one finds there what might be called a very good society stock company—an exceptional number, in fact, of agreeable people, intimate acquaintance with whom is rarely formed except in youth, unless subsequently by chance encounter in Europe. When thus casually met, they are apt to emerge from their social shells in curiously attractive shapes and phases. Socially, however, the trouble with Boston is that there is no current of fresh outside life everlastingly flowing in and passing out. It is, so to speak, stationary—a world, a Boston world, unto itself. The winter climate of Boston is distinctly Arctic, and society life, from sympathy, perhaps, seems then to pass through a long period of cold storage.

The worst wrench, and by far the most painful one, was in the case of Quincy. That was awful! Quincy was bone of my bone—flesh of the Adams flesh. There I had lived vicariously or in person since 1640; there on my return from the war I had made my home, and later (1870) built my house; there I had fought my fight, not unsuccessfully, through the best years of life; there my children were born; in fact, I felt as if I owned the town, for every part of it was familiar to me, and it was I who had recounted its history. I felt about it exactly as Hawthorne felt about Salem. In his inimitable introductory chapter to the *Scarlet Letter*, he says: 'This old town—my native place [I, by the way, was born in Boston; but Quincy, none the less, was my race-place] though I have dwelt much away from it, both in boyhood and mature years—possesses, or did possess, a hold on my affections, the force of which I have never realized during my seasons of actual residence there. It is now nearly two centuries and a quarter since the original Briton, the earliest emigrant of my name, made his appearance in the wild and forest-bordered settlement, which has since become a city. And here his descendants have been born and died, and have mingled their earthly substance with the soil; until no small portion of it must necessarily be akin to the mortal frame wherewith, for a little while, I walk the streets. In part, therefore, the attachment which I speak of is the mere sensuous sympathy of dust for dust. So has it been in my case. I felt it almost a destiny to make Salem my home. Nevertheless, this very sentiment is evidence that the connection, which has become an unhealthy one, should at last be severed. Human nature will not flourish, any more than a potato, if it be planted and replanted, for too long a series of generations, in the same worn-out soil.'

Early one Monday morning in the latter part of November, 1893, I mounted my horse at the door of my house on the hill at Quincy—the sun being hardly above the horizon of the distant sea-line in the nipping atmosphere—and rode over to Lincoln. I have not passed a night at Quincy since.

I have never set foot on President's Hill since 1895, when I parted with the property. I never mean to again. The Quincy I knew has ceased to exist; and, with the present Quincy, I have neither ties nor sympathy. In fact, I never now go there without, as I come away, drawing a breath of deep relief. When I enter it, I seem going into a tomb; when I leave it, getting back to Lincoln, it is a return to the sunlight and living air.

CHARLES FRANCIS ADAMS
An Autobiography, Boston and New York, 1916.

THE FUNERAL OF EMILY DICKINSON

May 19, 1886

To Amherst to the funeral of that rare and strange creature, Emily Dickinson.

The country exquisite, day perfect, and an atmosphere of its own, fine and strange, about the whole house and grounds—a more saintly and elevated 'House of Usher.' The grass of the lawn full of buttercups, violets and wild geranium; in house a handful of pansies and another of lilies of valley on piano.

E.D.'s face a wondrous restoration of youth—she is fifty-four and looked thirty, not a gray hair or wrinkle, and perfect peace on the beautiful brow. There was a little bunch of violets at the neck and one pink *Cypripedium;* the sister Vinnie put in two heliotropes by her hand 'to take to Judge Lord.' I read a poem by Emily Brontë.

How large a portion of the people who have most interested me have passed away.

COLONEL THOMAS WENTWORTH HIGGINSON, 1886.

Richard Cory

Whenever Richard Cory went down town,
We people on the pavement looked at him:
He was a gentleman from sole to crown,
Clean favored, and imperially slim.

And he was always quietly arrayed,
And he was always human when he talked;
But still he fluttered pulses when he said,
'Good-morning,' and he glittered when he walked.

And he was rich—yes, richer than a king—
And admirably schooled in every grace:
In fine, we thought that he was everything
To make us wish that we were in his place.

So on we worked, and waited for the light,
And went without the meat, and cursed the bread;
And Richard Cory, one calm summer night,
Went home and put a bullet through his head.

EDWIN ARLINGTON ROBINSON
Children of the Night, 1897.

Cornish, Maine, Sunday, December 23, 1934

Dear Friend,

I feel sorry that I couldn't have sent your present before Christmas. I want to tell you I have been sick about three weeks. I have the croup just like a baby. Nights I have to get up and build a fire and set my feet in the oven, the cold air makes me cough so. I am just as weak as a rag.

Well, the pig dressed 420 lbs. We have a beef creature to kill later, and if the little potatoes hold out, I think we can winter. We have a very little snow that came yesterday. We got enough out of our sweet corn to pay our tax and $1.35 left so you see what a lot of work we done to stay in Cornish a year. Remember me to the rest of the folks and excuse writing—for I am a poor hand to write to the girls. I wish you was down here to help eat the pig.

January 12, 1935

I am alone this evening. My brother has gone to grange meeting. I am feeling a lot better than I did. We have such changes in the weather no wonder any one is sick. Last Sunday they plowed the roads by here. It took from 1 o'clock till 4 to get over to the gate with the snowplow and 5 men shovelling. Jan 1st we got 16 in. of snow and the wind blew about a week—filled the road full. But the rain lately has carried it most all off. Over in the pasture it looks like summer. We got up a little wood on the snow. I haven't had a sleigh ride yet.

Perhaps you may think I am old fashion, but I wish things in the country were same as they used to be in years past, before autos got so plenty. Then you could see 18 or 20 yoke oxen all in one string. Farmers could haul wood to market. Folks could break colts. You could hear sleigh bells.

Today every poor Creature that's got $10 has got an auto. I have been today to see a fellow that owes me $5. I couldn't get a cent but he runs a car. There never was such times around here. Poor families. Little kids. I often think of some around here when I am putting wood into the stove, nice dry wood. Lots gets it all ice. I don't see how they keep warm.

Well I guess I will sign off and drink a quart of milk and go to bed. Please write and keep well this winter, for I want you to go to meeting with me in May.

Love to all,
Ed Pendexter

excuse writing

Letters to Nancy Newhall.

Ebb

An Old Man's Winter Night

All out of doors looked darkly in at him
Through the thin frost, almost in separate stars,
That gathers on the pane in empty rooms.
What kept his eyes from giving back the gaze
Was the lamp tilted near them in his hand.
What kept him from remembering what it was
That brought him to that creaking room was age.
He stood with barrels round him—at a loss.
And having scared the cellar under him
In clomping there, he scared it once again
In clomping off;—and scared the outer night,
Which has its sounds, familiar, like the roar
Of trees and crack of branches, common things,
But nothing so like beating on a box.
A light he was to no one but himself
Where now he sat, concerned with he knew what,
A quiet light, and then not even that.
He consigned to the moon, such as she was,
So late-arising, to the broken moon
As better than the sun in any case
For such a charge, his snow upon the roof,
His icicles along the wall to keep;
And slept. The dog that shifted with a jolt
Once in the stove, disturbed him and he shifted,
And eased his heavy breathing, but still slept.
One aged man—one man—can't fill a house,
A farm, a countryside, or if he can,
It's thus he does it of a winter night.

ROBERT FROST, 1936

2   *Tenacious Roots*

LETTERS FROM PROUT'S NECK, MAINE

Winter

I have just put coal on the fire, which accounts for this smut. I made a mistake in not getting a larger stove. It is very comfortable within ten feet of it. It heats the room within two feet of the floor, & water freezes anywhere within that space. I wear rubber boots & two pair of drawers. I know very well what a mistake I am making. I should 'simply irritate my skin & take a cold bath.' But water is scarce. I take a sponge & pick out certain portions of my body which I do at any time of tide, & always. I break four inches of ice to get my water. I thank the Lord for this opportunity for reflection. P.S. Great storm last night. Cold as the d----.

Spring

Things are looking very beautiful here today. I had my place covered with seaweed last winter & now it is raked off just before this rain it is as green as Central Park. I have raw Bermuda onions & *young* dandelions every day. Do not waist [sic] so much on appearances you do not live well enough you do not eat enough or drink enough. I brought down Leg of Canada Mutton, two Spring Chickens, Bermuda onions, six bottles old rum, one Edam cheese, six bottles of rare old vatted whiskey 'good as the Bank of England,' put up by S.S.P., Boston pilot bread. You see I can afford to live better than you can, as I cut off servants that mean all these good things—each extra *one* means about three legs of mutton, which you go without & eat corned beef & cabbage.

Return from Boston

When I got home about 1 o'clock I opened my fish & cooked two shad roes & cut up a cucumber in cold water —then, with a quart of South Side Scarboro cider, I knew that I was again in my own house. When I am away from here I am obliged to sleep on the edge of the bed frame in order to get a nap as all the Hotel beds are too soft and stale.

A Christmas Present of Wine

I have proof that there is something fine in that wine, as I had taken a glass & was peeling vegetables for my dinner & thinking of the painting that I had just finished, & singing with a very loud voice, See! the Conquering Hero come [sic], & I sung it, Sound the *Parsnip*, beat the Drum!

Refusing a Visitor

There is a *large boat* in one of my two rooms, the only rooms now in commission. *I have no studio*, my water is turned off from the sand pipe [sic], and I regret sincerely to say that I cannot receive a visit from you at this time of year even for a day. My own brothers know better than to come down here. Next Summer if we live I will without fail let you know when the hotels are open & invite you out here & you will find a very beautiful spot & a hearty welcome from me.

    I deny that I am a recluse as is generally understood by that term. Neither am I an unsociable hog. I wrote you its true that it was not convenient to receive a visitor, that was to save you as well as myself. Since you must know it I have never yet had a bed in my house. I do my own work. No other man or woman within half a mile & four miles from railroad & P.O. This is the only life in which I am permitted to mind my own business. I suppose I am today the only man in New England who can do it. I am perfectly happy and contented. Happy New Year.

MAINE FISHERMEN

You might see him standing on the pebble beach or in a fish-house doorway. He was one of the small company of elderly, gaunt-shaped great fishermen whom I used to like to see leading up a deep-laden boat by the head, as if it were a horse, from the water's edge to the steep slope of the pebble beach. There was an alliance and understanding between them, so close that it was apparently speechless. They gave much time to watching one another's boats go out or come in; they lent a ready hand at tending one another's lobster traps in rough weather; they helped to clean the fish or to sliver porgies for the trawls; and when a boat came in from deep-sea fishing they were never far out of the way, and hastened to help carry it ashore, two by two, splashing alongside. No boat could help being steady and way-wise under their instant direction and companionship.

These ancient seafarers had houses and lands not outwardly different from other Dunnet Landing dwellings, and two of them were fathers of families, but their true dwelling places were the sea, and the stony beach that edged its familiar shore, and the fish-houses, where much salt brine from the mackerel kits had soaked the very timbers into a state of brown permanence and petrification.

WINSLOW HOMER
SARAH ORNE JEWETT
The Country of the Pointed Firs, 1896.

By the Morning Boat

On the coast of Maine, where many green islands and salt inlets fringe the deep-cut shore line; where balsam firs and bayberry bushes send their fragrance far seaward, and song-sparrows sing all day, and the tide runs plashing in and out among the weedy ledges; where cowbells tinkle on the hills and herons stand in the shady coves—on the lonely coast of Maine stood a small gray house facing the morning light. All the weather-beaten houses of that region face the sea apprehensively, like the women who live in them.

SARAH ORNE JEWETT
Atlantic Monthly, October, 1890.

Jedidy and the Devil

'I got to be gittin' m' ghost-legs on,' said Captain Jedidy Cole as he rose from his Burying Box, opened one eye and saw the Devil coming along Captain's Row. 'I got to be sailin' along o' the tide. Goodbye, Sairy Ann. I'll see you, come Judgment.'

'Here I be, Jedidy,' said the Devil, just outside the door.

'Gimme ten minutes' start,' pleaded the Captain, 'ten minutes and m' bowie knife.'

'You don't desarve it,' said the Devil, 'but on account you're a marryin' man; four times, ain't it, Jedidy? One in Hongkong and two in Cadiz—I don't rightly place the third.'

'She was an error,' admitted the Captain. 'She wa'n't our kind.'

'Son,' said the Devil, 'I was always tender-hearted of you. I'll give you ten minutes and your bowie knife, but it ain't no use, poor old Jedidy. I kin run faster than a coon-cat scootin', and you ain't hardly got your ghost-legs on.'

'You leave me be,' said Jedidy. 'You made your bargain. I don't say you don't desarve me. Faithful you bin, and steadfast persued me, ever since I was knee-high. But ten minutes and a bowie knife it is; ten minutes I'll take.'

'Light up your binnacles and set your course,' directed the Devil. 'I'm countin' up to ten.'

Jedidy Cole blew out four corpse-candles and tucked them under his Grave Bonnet. Then he speeded over to the pumpkin field, cut four pumpkins by the stumps, ripped off a reefingyard of shroud, and quick knotted three of the pumpkins over his shoulder. He cut two eyes, a nose and a grinning mouth in the fourth pumpkin, stuck it on top of a picket in the fence, and went down to Hawes Tavern to get a rum bracer for his ghost-legs.

By and by the Devil, who was slow at numbers, counted as far as ten. 'Hie, Cap'n,' he called, 'I see you hidin' in the beanfield yonder. Grin now. You won't grin long! I'm a-comin' after you!' As he drew alongside the pumpkin, he grew more talkative. 'Lookie, Jedidy,' he confided to the pumpkin, 'I never did approve of you given' out three grams of grog a day, and orange after cod-muddle.'

Old Jedidy, who was used to having the Devil right at his elbow, heard that insult down in Hawes Tavern, forgot he was dead, and spoke right up just as he used to do when his soul was safe in his body.

'Drat your hide,' swore Jedidy. 'You're makin' me out a fresh-water Cap'n.'

'Yo-ho-noddle,' sung the Devil, 'I might have knowed you'd be down in thet Tavern.' He turned to the pumpkin. 'Beg pardon, Sir,' he said. 'I took you for somebuddy wiser.'

'Ever since I bin dead,' Jedidy chided himself, 'I bin actin' nit-wit, like a fust mate. Here I wasted one good punkin, and only three left over.'

'Watch me, I'm a-comin',' yelled the Devil, who always thought himself the whole crow's nest and the ship's clock as well.

Captain Jedidy whipped out his bowie, pulled a corpse-drip from under his bonnet, carved a pumpkin from his pack, then skewered the face on the chairback in the tavern. He lit the drip inside the pumpkin and chucked it under the whiskers. 'Now I'll be movin' on,' said he. 'You let the Old Man have his way. Don't you go interruptin' him.'

Jedidy cloud-floated through the window; the Devil sidled through the door. The Devil sat down beside the pumpkin, drank a round of ale and told his listener all that they two were going to do when they got home. Fifth drink around, the Devil grew suspicious. It wasn't natural for Jedidy not to be answering back. So the Devil decided to bait him a little. 'Down home,' said he, 'I got your two wives from Cadiz, waitin' to communicate.' The pumpkin said nothing. But old Jedidy who was making his way from Chatham to Orleans, going fast on his new ghost-legs, heard him, way back in Hawes Tavern, telling about the ladies from Cadiz.

'Drat your hide, thet's a lie,' roared Jedidy. 'One of them wives went into a nun-house. She's salted down fer heaven.'

'Yo-ho-noddle,' sung the Devil. 'I thought you was unnatural silent. But never you mind, I'm a-comin' after you up there in Eastham South Parish. I'll be a-treadin' stern-water before you port your helm.'

'Now I've done it,' sighed old Jedidy, who was resting in Treat's Burying Lot. 'Wasted another punkin.' He drew out his bowie knife, carved a face, lit it with a corpse-candle, and set the pumpkin on top of an urn-shaped stone. 'You bide there,' said Jedidy, 'and don't go answerin' questions.'

In no time at all the Devil arrived in Eastham South Parish, where he came upon the pumpkin sitting on top of a white tombstone in Old Man Treat's Burying Acre.

'Jedidy,' said the Devil to the pumpkin, 'you make a fine spook. Your figger has curves to it. You ain't a-tall the barrel you was.'

Jedidy, scuttling through North Parish, nearly yelled back an answer; then chuckled to himself. 'This time, Old Feller,' said he, 'you're not a-goin' to ketch me.' He made fast time along Nauset Plain and ran into Wellfleet. By and by the Devil, getting playful, poked his friend in the ribs, 'Ai-ouch!' yelled the Old Man, sucking his finger. 'You're as hard as nails, old Jedidy, just like you always was. What keeps your muscle up?'

Way past Wellfleet, Jedidy thought he'd die of a chuckle-spasm. 'Lan' sakes,' he giggled, 'I use Jamaica rum. Thet sulphur you drink keeps a man lack-a-daisy.'

Far off he was, but the Devil heard as the Devil always hears when anyone speaks to him directly. 'Looky, you lan'-lummox,' he swore, abusing the pumpkin, 'you go unner groun' till Judgment. This ain't your watch.' He gave the tombstone a shove. The pumpkin rolled down, broke on the ground. The candle guttered out.

'Hell's bells,' said the Devil, impressed. 'Kin I destroy the Lord's deceased like thet?' He swung his bright cloak wide and handsome and in a run-o-bluefish hurry started for Wellfleet Village.

'Sufferin' scat,' groaned the anxious Captain as he lighted his last candle. 'I'm down to m' boat-rations now.' He climbed up the Tree-before-the-Moors, the last big oak, north of Wellfleet, and lodged the lighted pumpkin face on the skysail yard of the oak. Then he climbed down and hurried on. In no time, the Devil was alongside the tree. 'Howdy-doo,' said he, craning his neck, 'I see you hidin' on the top-boom, Jedidy. Come down, or I'll be after you.' The pumpkin did not move. The Devil was loath to climb a tree, for the air was angel-moorings. Any cloud-floating or tree-climbing made the Devil sick.

'Aw, come down, Jedidy,' he coaxed. 'I'll let you have another rum-hot before we go home.'

The lighted face grinned. 'Yo-ho-noddle,' sung the Devil, formal and dignified. 'Watch me git you!' He swarmed up the ratlines, passed the topgallant yard, passed the top royals, clear up to the skysail yard. As he reached the smiling pumpkin, he slipped; the lighted face rolled to the ground; the Devil swung by his pants.

'Ha-ha,' roared Jedidy, over past Truro. 'Lookit you goin' up to heaven!' Against the sky, Jedidy far away, could see the Devil swinging.

'So thet's where you be,' said the squirming Devil. 'Wait

Tenacious Roots

till I open up m' hind pocket and git m' flint undid.' No sooner said than accomplished. The Devil set his black Paris pants afire, burned himself free of the oak-tree branch, dropped to the ground, and smothered the fire by sitting down on it. Jedidy was racing into Provincetown with his Bier Bonnet gone and his Grave Jacket torn into strips. In no time at all the Devil was behind him.

'I give up,' said old Jedidy. 'You're a habit with me, just like likker. It ain't in me to git away from you. Lead on, mate, I'll be goin' wherever you take me.'

'Lead on?' said the Devil, perplexed. 'Ain't we got to Provincetown? Ain't we to home?'

Cape Cod folk tale, as told by Elizabeth Reynard, in *The Narrow Land*, 1934.

WALK IN BOSTON

I have been in Boston the whole blest morning, toted around by the Wards, who had as usual asked me to dine with them. I, as it turned out, found myself in for following the innocent lamb Lily up and down the town for two hours, to hold bundles and ring bells for her. Clear sharp cold morning, thermometer 5 degrees at sunrise, and the streets covered with one glare of ice. I had thick smooth shoes and went sliding off like an avalanche every three steps, while she, having india-rubbers and being a Bostonian, went ahead like a swan. I had among other things to keep her bundles from harm, to wipe away every three minutes the trembling jewel with which the cold *would* with persistent kindness ornament my coral nose; to keep a hypocritic watchful eye on her movements lest she fall; to raise my hat gracefully to more and more of her acquaintances every block; to skate round and round embracing lamp-posts and door-scrapers by the score to keep from falling, as well as to avoid serving old-lady promenaders in the same way; to cut capers 4 feet high at the rate of 20 a second, every now and then, for the same purpose; to keep from scooting off down hills and round corners as fast as my able-bodied companion; often to do all of these at once and then fall lickety-bang like a chandelier, but when so to preserve an expression of placid beatitude or easy nonchalance despite the raging fiend within: oh it beggars description! When finally it was over and I stood alone I shook my companion's dust from my feet and, biting my beard with rage, sware a mighty oath unto high heaven that I would never, while reason held her throne in this distracted orb, *never,* NEVER, by word, look or gesture and this without mental reservation acknowledge a 'young lady' as a human being.

WILLIAM JAMES
Letter to his family, Christmas, 1861.

Tenacious Roots

Winter and Summer, cold and heat, town and country, force and freedom, marked two modes of life and thought, balanced like lobes of the brain. Town was winter, confinement, school, rule, discipline; straight, gloomy streets, piled with six feet of snow in the middle; frosts that made the snow sing under wheels or runners; thaws when the streets became dangerous to cross; society of uncles, aunts, and cousins who expected children to behave themselves and who were not always gratified; above all else, winter represented the desire to escape and go free. Town was restraint, law, unity. Country, only seven miles away, was liberty, diversity, outlawry, the endless delight of mere sense impressions given by nature for nothing, and breathed by boys without knowing it.

Boys are wild animals, rich in the treasures of sense, but the New England boy had a wider range of emotions than boys of more equable climates. He felt his nature crudely, as it was meant. To the boy Henry Adams, summer was drunken. Among senses, smell was the strongest—smell of hot pine-woods and sweet fern in the scorching summer noons; of new-mown hay; of ploughed earth; of box hedges; of peaches, lilacs, syringas; of stables, barns, cowyards; of salt water and low tide on the marshes. Whether the children rolled in the grass, or waded in the brooks, or swam in the salt ocean, or sailed in the bay, or fished for smelts in the creeks, or netted minnows in the salt marshes, or took to the pine-woods and the granite quarries, or chased muskrats and hunted snapping turtles in the swamps, or mushrooms or nuts in the autumn hills, summer and country were always sensual living.

HENRY ADAMS
The Education of Henry Adams, 1918.

A PAINTING BY RYDER

Just some sea, some clouds, and a sail boat on the tossing waters. I knew little or nothing about Albert Ryder then, and when I learned he was from New England the same feeling came over me in the given degree as came out of the Emerson's Essays when they were first given to me—I felt as if I had read a page of the Bible. All my essential Yankee qualities were brought forth out of this picture and if I needed to be stamped American this was the first picture that had done this—for it had in it everything that I knew and had experienced about my own New England—even though I had never lived by the sea—it had in it the stupendous solemnity of a Blake mystical picture and it had a sense of realism besides that bore such a force of nature itself as to leave me breathless. The picture had done its work and I was a convert to the field of imagination into which I was born. I had been thrown back into the body and being of my own country as by no other influence that had come to me.

* * * * *

A gull flies high
And sun gleams catch
His whiteness
As he turns and soars.

He looks down on the sea
As on a pool that he commands
The waves a plaything
For his wings
And distant clouds
A cover for his love.

MARSDEN HARTLEY
MIRIAM COLWELL

The Nursery Rhyme and the Summer Visitor

Green Mountain Mary, Green Mountain Mary
What does your garden grow?

Violets, moss, ground pine, goldenrod, briars,
Strawberries, hardhack, wintergreen, ferns,
And a little bit of grass, alas.

Will you sell me your meadow?

                Oh, no.

Who crops it?

       Deer.

See here, Green Mountain Mary, you people are very,—
Excuse me—
Queer.

GENEVIEVE TAGGARD, 1945.

Lilacs

Lilacs
False blue,
White,
Purple,
Colour of lilac,
Your great puffs of flowers
Are everywhere in this my New England.
Among your heart-shaped leaves
Orange orioles hop like music-box birds and sing
Their little weak soft songs;
In the crooks of your branches
The bright eyes of song sparrows
   sitting on spotted eggs
Peer restlessly through the light and shadow
Of all Springs.
Lilacs in dooryards
Holding quiet conversations with an early moon;
Lilacs watching a deserted house
Settling sideways into the grass of an old road;
Lilacs, wind-beaten, staggering under a
   lopsided shock of bloom
Above a cellar dug into a hill.
You are everywhere.
You were everywhere.
You tapped the window when the preacher
   preached his sermon,
And ran along the road beside the boy
   going to school.
You stood by pasture-bars
   to give the cows good milking,
You persuaded the housewife
   that her dish pan was of silver
And her husband an image of pure gold.
You flaunted the fragrance of your blossoms
Through the wide doors of Custom Houses—
You, and sandal-wood, and tea,
Charging the noses of quill-driving clerks
When a ship was in from China.
You called to them: 'Goose-quill men,
   goose-quill men,
May is a month for flitting,'
Until they writhed on their high stools
And wrote poetry on their letter-sheets
   behind the propped-up ledgers.
Paradoxical New England clerks,
Writing inventories in ledgers,
   reading the 'Song of Solomon' at night,
So many verses before bed-time,
Because it was the Bible.
The dead fed you
Amid the slant stones of graveyards.
Pale ghosts who planted you
Came in the night-time
And let their thin hair blow
   through your clustered stems.
You are of the green sea,
And of the stone hills which reach a long distance.
You are of elm-shaded streets with little shops
   where they sell kites and marbles,
You are of great parks where everyone walks
   and nobody is at home.
You cover the blind sides of greenhouses
And lean over the top to say a hurry-word
   through the glass
To your friends, the grapes, inside.

Tenacious Roots

Lilacs,
False blue,
White,
Purple,
Colour of lilac,
You have forgotten your Eastern origin,
The veiled women with eyes like panthers,
The swollen, aggressive turbans of jeweled Pashas.
Now you are a very decent flower,
A reticent flower.
A curiously clear-cut, candid flower,
Standing beside clean doorways,
Friendly to a house-cat and a pair of spectacles,
Making poetry out of a bit of moonlight
And a hundred or two sharp blossoms.

Maine knows you,
Has for years and years;
New Hampshire knows you,
And Massachusetts
And Vermont.
Cape Cod starts you along the beaches
   to Rhode Island;
Connecticut takes you from a river to the sea.
You are brighter than apples,
Sweeter than tulips,
You are the great flood of our souls
Bursting above the leaf-shapes of our hearts,
You are the smell of all Summers,
The love of wives and children,
The recollection of the gardens of little children,

You are State Houses and Charters
And the familiar treading of the foot to and fro
   on a road it knows.
May is lilac here in New England,
May is a thrush singing 'Sun-up!' on a tip-top ash-tree,
May is white clouds behind pine-trees
Puffed out and marching upon a blue sky.
May is a green as no other,
May is much sun through small leaves,
May is soft earth,
And apple-blossoms,
And windows open to a South wind.
May is a full light wind of lilac
From Canada to Narragansett Bay.

Lilacs,
False blue,
White,
Purple,
Colour of lilac,
Heart-leaves of lilac all over New England,
Roots of lilac under all the soil of New England,
Lilac in me because I am New England,
Because my roots are in it,
Because my leaves are of it,
Because my flowers are for it,
Because it is my country
And I speak to it of itself
And sing of it with my own voice
Since certainly it is mine.

AMY LOWELL, 1925.

JOURNEY TO THE NORTH

It was his train and it had come to take him to the strange and secret heart of the great North that he had never known, but whose austere and lonely image, whose frozen heat and glacial fire, and dark stern beauty had blazed in his vision since he was a child. For he had dreamed and hungered for the proud unknown North with that wild ecstasy, that intolerable and wordless joy of longing and desire, which only a Southerner can feel. With a heart of fire, a brain possessed, a spirit haunted by the strange, secret and unvisited magic of the proud North, he had always known that some day he should find it—his heart's hope and his father's country, the lost but unforgotten half of his own soul,—and take it for his own.

Here was the passionate enigma of New England felt: New England, with its harsh and stony soil, and its tragic and lonely beauty; its desolate rocky coasts and its swarming fisheries, the white, piled, frozen bleakness of its winters with the magnificent jewelry of stars, the dark firwoods, and the warm little white houses at which it is impossible to look without thinking of groaning bins, hung bacon, hard cider, succulent bastings, and love's warm, white, and opulent flesh, always the buried heart, the sunken passion, the frozen heat. And then, after the long, unendurably hard-locked harshness of the frozen winter, the coming of spring as now, like a lyrical cry, like a flicker of rain across a window glass, like the sudden and delicate noises of a spinet—the coming of spring and ecstasy, and over night the thrum of wings, the burst of the tender buds, the ripple and dance of the roughened water, the light of flowers, the sudden, fleeting, almost captured, and exultant spring.

THOMAS WOLFE
Of Time and the River, New York, 1935.

3   *Affirmations*

To Ethan Allen

Sleep, Ethan, where you belong,
Allen of the little clan,
Clan of large men on lavish continent,
In the place of uncut trees and the trackless green.
Sleep to the thrush's tranquil, seasonal song.
Vermont itself is your big monument;
And also those who sing of wilderness and man;
Of intelligence and hardihood and the keen
Struggle. Song is for the heroes in their time of rest.
Sleep in your granite bed under the mountain tent,
Beside your lakes and rivers; near falls that splash and flare.
Daily your turbulent spirit delights this air.
Sleep well in your wedge-shaped bed,
Under the slanted snow, or in spring's frequent
Vehement thunder. Sleep. A poet said,
Nature is never spent.
Neither are we, nor were you, Old Heart of Oak.
I heard your tone when first the thunder spoke.
The toil of men and women, the excited feet
Stamping at country dances, and Town Meeting Day
Chiming their biblical notes of *yea* and *nay,*
And many customs sweet
Prolong an enduring impulse this citizen took
To be his passion: to be Freedom's servant rude.
A man no Tory conclave could undo,
Founding a state and writing a troubled book.
Prisoner, Freeman, leader and strategist,
Sagacious creature with uplifted fist
Against all tyrants... Those who remember you
Wish never to outgrow such servitude.
Sleep, Ethan Allen of the little clan,
Vermont in its quiet way recalls this man.
Sleep, Ethan, in the mountains where you belong.
Sleep to the thrush's tranquil, seasonal song.

GENEVIEVE TAGGARD
A Part of Vermont, 1945.

Affirmations

I think that, as life is action and passion, it is required of a man that he should share the passion and action of his time at peril of being judged not to have lived.

Accidents may call up the events of the war. You see a battery of guns go by at a trot, and for a moment you are back at White Oak Swamp, or Antietam, or on the Jerusalem Road. You hear a few shots fired in the distance, and for an instant your heart stops as you say to yourself, the skirmishers are at it, and listen for the long roll of fire from the main line. You meet an old comrade after many years; he recalls the moment when you were nearly surrounded by the enemy, and again there comes up to you that swift and cunning thinking on which once hung life or freedom—Shall I stand the best chance if I try the pistol or the sabre on that man who means to stop me? Will he get his carbine free before I reach him, or can I kill him first? These and the thousand other events we have known are called up, I say, by accident, and, apart from accident, they lie forgotten.

But as surely as this day comes round we are in the presence of the dead. For one hour at least, on this day when we decorate their graves, the dead come back and live with us. I see them now, more than I can number, as once I saw them on this earth. They are the same bright figures, or their counterparts, that come also before your eyes; and when I speak of those who were my brothers, the same words describe yours.

For the Puritan still lives in New England, thank God! and will live there so long as New England lives and keeps her old renown. New England is not dead yet. She still is mother of a race of conquerors,— stern men, little given to the expression of their feelings, sometimes careless of the graces, but fertile, tenacious, and knowing only duty. Each of you, as I do, thinks of a hundred such that he has known.

I see one—grandson of a hard rider of the Revolution and bearer of his historic name—who was with us at Fair Oaks, and afterwards for five days and nights in front of the enemy the only sleep that he would take was what he could snatch sitting erect in his uniform and resting his back against a hut. He fell at Gettysburg. His brother, a surgeon, who rode, as our surgeons so often did, wherever the troops would go, I saw kneeling in ministration to a wounded man just in rear of our line at Antietam, his horse's bridle round his arm,—the next moment his ministrations were ended. There is one who on this day is always present to my mind. He entered the army at nineteen, a second lieutenant. In the Wilderness, already at the head of his regiment, he fell, using the moment that was left to him of life, to give all his little fortune to his soldiers. I saw him in camp, on the march, in action, and never did I see him fail to choose that alternative of conduct which was most disagreeable to himself. He was indeed a Puritan in all his virtues, without the Puritan austerity.

Not all of those with whom we once stood shoulder to shoulder—not all of those whom we once loved and revered—are gone. On this day we still meet our companions in the freezing winter bivouacs and in those dreadful summer marches where every faculty of the soul seemed to depart one after another, leaving only a dumb animal power to set the teeth and to persist—a blind belief that somewhere and at last there was rest and water.

We know very well that we cannot live in associations with the past alone, and that, if we would be worthy of the past, we must find new fields for action or thought, and make for ourselves new careers.

Through our great good fortune, in our youth our hearts were touched with fire. It was given to us to learn at the outset that life is a profound and passionate thing.

JUSTICE OLIVER WENDELL HOLMES
Dead, yet Living, an address delivered on Memorial Day, 1884, at Keene, New Hampshire, before the John Sedgwick Post No. 4, Grand Army of the Republic.

To His Son, Dante

Charlestown State Prison, August 18, 1927

If nothing happens, they will electrocute us right after midnight, on August 22nd. Therefore, here I am, right with you with love and with open heart as ever I was yesterday.

Don't cry, Dante, because many tears have been wasted, as your mother's have been wasted, for seven years, and never did any good. So, Son, instead of crying be strong, be brave, so as to be able to comfort your mother, and when you want to distract your mother from the discouraging soulness, I will tell you what I used to do. To take her for a long walk in the quiet country, gathering wild flowers here and there, resting under the shade of trees, between the harmony of the vivid stream and the gentle tranquility of the mothernature, and I am sure she will enjoy this very much, as you surely would be happy for it. But remember, Dante, in the play of happiness, don't you use all for yourself only, but down yourself just one step, at your side, and help the weak ones that cry for help, help the persecuted and the victim, because they are your better friends; they are the comrades that fight and fall as your father and Bartolo fought and fell yesterday for the conquest of the joy of freedom for all. In the struggle of life you will find more love and you will be loved.

After Receiving Sentence of Death

April 9, 1927, at Dedham, Massachusetts

If it had not been for these thing, I might have live out my life talking at street corners to scorning men. I might have die, unmarked, unknown, a failure. Now we are not a failure. This is our career and our triumph. Never in our full life could we hope to do such work for tolerance, for joostice, for man's understanding of man as now we do by accident. Our words—our lives—our pains—nothing! The taking of our lives—lives of a good shoemaker and a poor fishpeddler—all! That last moment belongs to us—that agony is our triumph.

NICOLA SACCO
BARTOLOMEO VANZETTI

Affirmations

I dream of a world of infinite and invaluable variety; in human variety in height and weight, color and skin, hair and nose and lip. And far above and beyond this in a realm of true freedom: in thought and dream, fantasy and imagination: in gift, aptitude and genius—all possible manner of difference, topped with freedom of soul to do and be, and freedom of thought to give to a world and build with it, all wealth of inborn individuality. Each effort to stop this freedom is a blow at democracy—that real democracy which is reservoir and opportunity and the fight against which is murdering civilization. There can be no perfect democracy curtailed by color, race or poverty. But with all, we accomplish all, even Peace.

There will be time later when the horsemen of Apocalypse ride in from the quadrants of the earth
And pull up by a misty woods back of an old battleground;
And the one whose name is Conquest will dismount, and he will break his bow upon his knee and trample it;
He will wipe blood from both hands on the hide of his snow-white horse, and turn, and fade into the mists.
And the one whose name is War will grasp his great sword by the hilt and circle it round his head
And fling it far, and it will shatter on the crosses of fallen soldiers.
And the dead young men will hear the sound, though their thoughts be distant and their bones be intersticed with grass.
And the saddle of the red horse shall be empty.
And the one called Famine will drop his balances, remembering the look of the rich wheatfields upon the way, and he too will alight, and skulk into the darkest shadows of the woods, taking care to avoid the barest touch of the seeds of the meanest fruit;
And only the rider by the name of Death will sit still on the pale horse, and listen for sounds in the wind, and turn away in the direction of the west,
Leaving the riderless horses to graze forever on substances of night.

W. E. BURGHARDT DU BOIS
The World and Africa, 1947.

NORMAN CORWIN
On a Note of Triumph, 1945.

Affirmations

Three hundred years: in time's eye only a moment...
Time only for the single dream,
as, in this misty morning, all our generations seem:
seem only one, one face, one hope, one name:
those who first crossed the sea, first came,
and the new born grandchild, crying, one and the same.
Yes now, now most of all, in the fateful glare
of mankind's hatred everywhere,
time yields its place, with its own bell
uncharms and then recharms its spell:
and time is gone, but everything else is here,
all is clear, all is one day, one year,
the many generations seem,
and are, one single purpose, one single name and dream...

CONRAD AIKEN, 1945.

The most refractory Westerner was willing to grant the old, proud boast of Massachusetts, that it had surpassed many empires in its contributions to progress and in its great men; and the nation could not forget New England, could not let the subject drop,—Americans could do anything but leave it alone. They like to tease New England, but they were never indifferent to it.

New England haunted the minds of Americans, who tried to read its riddle, as if for their souls' good they must know what it meant. What was the truth about it?—and there were reasons for this obsession, for, generally speaking, Americans had a stake in New England. They were deeply implicated in it, as the seat of their deepest, their stoutest, their greatest tradition. Their blood was mixed perhaps with other strains, and perhaps they had long lived in other regions, but New England was their ark of the covenant still. How fared this ark? Into what hands had it fallen? It meant much to Americans that this old region should fare well, as their palladium of truth, justice, freedom, and learning. They could not rest until they were reconciled to it, and until it was reconciled to them.

VAN WYCK BROOKS
New England: Indian Summer, 1940.

Afterword

The collaboration of Paul Strand and Nancy Newhall that resulted in the original publication of this now-classic book began with the one-man retrospective exhibition of Strand's photographs at The Museum of Modern Art in New York in 1945. The newly formed Department of Photography planned as part of its program to hold major retrospective exhibitions and to publish scholarly catalogues of the work of photographers we considered to be the masters. As curator of photography, I extended an invitation to Paul Strand to inaugurate this series. He accepted. But before I could put the exhibition on the walls, the United States had become involved in World War II. I joined the Army Air Force and was assigned to duty overseas. Happily, my late wife Nancy was appointed acting curator for the duration of my military service and took over the direction of the show and the writing of the catalogue.

Strand expressed the desire to collaborate closely with the exhibition director. Thus, each photograph was selected by them both. When either felt it needful, Strand made new prints especially for the show. The sequencing of the photographs and the hanging of them on the gallery walls were also equally collaborative.

During the exhibition, Nancy recollected, "Paul Strand and I were having lunch in the Museum garden and discussing a proposal that he do a book on New England. 'What about the text, and who should do it?' 'Why, the New Englanders themselves,' said I. 'Melville and Hawthorne and Thoreau and Emily Dickinson—who better? And it shouldn't be hard,' said I rashly, 'to find what you need.'"

A publisher was found. Friends volunteered their help. The modest advance was doubled by a loan from Elizabeth Marshall, a friend of the Museum and photography. Ferdinand Reyher, the writer, interrupted his schedule to serve voluntarily as a consulting editor. Bernard DeVoto was a perceptive guide through the maze of documents and literary works from which the text was built. When the original publisher decided not to bring out the book, Philip Vaudrin of the Oxford University Press took over the contract and oversaw the publication of the first edition.

Nancy's estimate of the time required was indeed rash. Photographing and researching, printing negatives both old and new and editing the text, selecting and sequencing photographs, marrying words and images took most of the time of both collaborators over a period of four years —Paul on location in northern New England or in the darkroom; Nancy in libraries, especially the New York Public Library, the New York Society Library, and the Boston Athenaeum.

The collaboration was ideal, for both Paul and Nancy saw the book not as a portfolio of fine photographs nor as a literary anthology with illustrations, but rather they envisaged it as an integrated whole, in which the text and the images would reinforce one another. In a sense, they both sought a syntax related to cinematic structure. Nancy was a keen student of film, and Paul was a brilliant director, editor, and photographer of documentaries.

An insight into the creation of this book can be gained from the correspondence between Paul in the field and Nancy in the libraries. It is noteworthy that both frequently used the language of the motion-picture editor, to whom "cutting" is the act of assembling film images with dialogue.

On June 1, 1946, Nancy wrote Paul: "Made a rough cut of the material so far. Good in some places; tenuous in others. I suppose any cut will remain vague until all text and photographs are in, but I wanted to see how we are coming. If we follow our original idea—... a portrait shown through the great underlying themes of social and cultural development—we need many more images with concrete associations: the sea, the country, the people. As: an image of peace and loveliness—might be in common with elms, or rolling countryside with glimpse of town in summer... an image of vast prospects of—clouds, horizons.... An image—very difficult—to accompany the love of books and excitement of scholarship... More than these even, we need the power and vastness of the sea—a violent storm or ragged, clearing sunset, without contemporary boats in it. The bowsprit of an old schooner or Friendship sloop, if you can find one still alive, would help."

Paul answered from Prospect Harbor, Maine: "You give me large orders—some of them should go to the person whom my landlady refers to as 'The Old Man up there,' pointing in a general way toward the sky. The sea, for instance, only has its moments and you have to be around. Once since I have been here it was remarkable for 5 minutes.... However, I have exposed about 60 with the Deardorff 8 x 10 camera and a number of 5 x 6s. We'll be working mostly now on people before I leave. Also maybe we have an apple tree in bloom and some other growing things. The other day I spent an afternoon with beach grass, which is endlessly fascinating."

It was a privilege for me to look on as the book came together in its final sequence with the typed text and work prints placed in order in large ring binders. What Paul considered "work prints" were excellent, but they were surpassed by the final prints that he made for the engraving, which were of exhibition quality neatly mounted on gray cards of uniform size, each with hinged guard sheets of white paper.

The first edition was published by the Oxford University Press in October 1950. By then Paul was living in France. "Have you got it?" Nancy wrote him on publication day. "Do you hold it in your hand, at last? You said, during some of those dark days that by God it would be published. And it *is*. So now it's up to the public and may they adore it and get from it something of what we did and what we put in!" Paul answered: "Thanks for your letter which I was happy to get—so full of good words from you. Yes, I think we can all be content with *Time in New England* as something really accomplished, that reflects the way we worked and as the result of the work we did."

If there was any reservation on the part of the authors, it was only in the quality of the reproductions. I am sure that if they were to see this new edition, they would be greatly pleased, and would thank Michael Hoffman, editor-publisher, Richard Benson who made the printer's negatives, and the staff of Aperture for the loving care expended in its production.

BEAUMONT NEWHALL

Additional Source Notes

p. 23　Francis Higginson. "A True Relation of the Last Voyage to New England," 1629. In A. Young, *Chronicles of the First Planters of the Colony of Massachusetts Bay*. Little and Brown, Boston, 1846.

pp. 24, 32, 33, 49　William Bradford. *Of Plymouth Plantation*. Written between 1630 and 1650; first published in 1856 by the Massachusetts Historical Society in series IV, vol. III, of their *Collections*.

p. 29　John Winthrop. *The History of New England from 1630-1649*. Phelps and Farnham, Boston, 1825.

p. 35　Anne Bradstreet. "The Flesh and the Spirit." *Works*. Abram E. Cutter, Charlestown, 1867.

p. 63　The Reverend Jonathan Edwards. *Works*, vol. I. S. Converse, New York, 1829-30.

p. 67　Judge Samuel Sewall. *Diary*. In Massachusetts Historical Society *Collections*, series V, vol. V, 1878-82.

p. 69　*Records and Files of the Quarterly Court of Essex County, Massachusetts*, vol. II, 1656-62. Essex Institute, Salem, 1912.

p. 75　Margaret Jacobs. Quoted by Charles W. Upham, Jr. in *Lectures on Witchcraft*. Boston, 1831.

p. 84　Sarah Kemble Knight. Private journal kept on a journey from Boston to New York in the year 1704. Frank H. Little, Albany, 1865.

p. 88　Henry Reed Stiles. *Bundling, Its Origin, Progress, and Decline in America*. Reprinted by Peter Pauper Press, Mt. Vernon, N.Y., 1937.

p. 94　John Adams. *Diary*. In *Works*, vol. II. Little and Brown, Boston, 1850. "A Son of Liberty." Quoted by M. C. Tyler in *The Literary History of the American Revolution*, vol. I. G. P. Putnam's Sons, New York, 1897.

pp. 96, 98　John Adams. *Works*, vol. IX. Little and Brown, Boston, 1850.

p. 99　Samuel Adams. *Writings*, vol. III. G. P. Putnam's Sons, New York and London, 1906.

p. 102.　Paul Revere. Letter to Reverend Jeremy Belknap, 1775. Massachusetts Historical Society.

p. 104.　Ephraim Banks. *Diary*. Quoted by Howard Fast in "Anniversary," *New Masses*, July 9, 1946.

p. 108　Henry W. De Puy. *Ethan Allen and the Green Mountain Heroes of '76*. Dayton and Wentworth, Boston, 1853.

p. 108　Abigail Adams. *Familiar Letters of John Adams and his Wife Abigail Adams during the Revolution*. Hurd and Houghton, New York, 1876.

p. 109　John Adams. Letter to Timothy Pickering, August 6, 1822, *Works*, vol. II. Little and Brown, Boston, 1850-56.

p. 112　Samuel Davis. Massachusetts Historical Society, *Proceedings*, 1869-70. Boston, 1871.

p. 113　Reverend Nathan Perkins. *A Narrative of a Tour through the State of Vermont*. The Elm Tree Press, Woodstock, Vt., 1920.

p. 116　Eliza Southgate Bowne. *A Girl's Life Eighty Years Ago*. Charles Scribner's Sons, New York, 1887.

p. 117　Lucy Larcom. *A New England Girlhood*. Houghton Mifflin Co., Boston, New York and Chicago, 1889.

p. 120　Seba Smith. *Life and Writings of Major Jack Downing of Downingville, State of Maine*. Lily, Wait, Colman and Holden, Boston, 1833.

p. 121　Elihu Burritt. *Diary*. Quoted by Merle Curtis in *The Learned Blacksmith*. Wilson-Erickson, Inc., New York, 1937.

p. 122　Ralph Waldo Emerson. *Lectures and Biographical Sketches*. Houghton Mifflin Co., Boston and New York, 1883.

p. 126　Ralph Waldo Emerson. *Lectures and Biographical Sketches*. Houghton Mifflin Co., Boston and New York, 1883.

p. 127　Seargent Smith Prentiss. "An Address to the New England Society of New Orleans." Quoted by G. L. Prentiss in *A Memoir of S.S. Prentiss*. Charles Scribner, New York, 1855.

p. 129　"Advice" and "Cargoes." Quoted by Ralph D. Paine in *Ships and Sailors of Old Salem*. Outing Publishing Co., New York, 1909.

p. 133　The record of fifteen clipper ships: compiled from Carl C. Cutler, *Greyhounds of the Sea*. G. P. Putnam's Sons, New York, 1930.

p. 134　Richard Henry Dana, Jr. *Two Years Before the Mast*. Harper and Brothers, New York, 1840.

p. 134　Herman Melville. Letter to Evert Duyckinck. Quoted by Willard Thorp in *Herman Melville*. American Book Co., New York, 1938.

pp. 135, 163　Herman Melville. *Moby Dick, or the Whale*. Harper and Brothers, New York, 1851.

p. 140　Obed Macy. *The History of Nantucket*. Hilliard Gray and Co., Boston, 1835.

p. 140　Owen Chase. *Narrative of the Most Extraordinary and Distressing Shipwreck of the Whale Ship Essex*. W. B. Gilley, New York, 1821.

p. 142　Reverend William Bentley. *Diary*. Quoted by Ralph D. Paine in *Ships and Sailors of Old Salem*. Outing Publishing Co., New York, 1909.

p. 144　Richard Henry Dana, Jr. *Two Years Before the Mast*. Harper and Brothers, New York, 1840.

p. 145　Ralph Waldo Emerson. "The Poet." *Essays, Second Series*. James Munroe and Co., Boston, 1854.

p. 146　Ralph Waldo Emerson. *Journals*. Houghton Mifflin Co., Boston and New York, 1911.

pp. 146, 148　Henry David Thoreau. *Walden*. Ticknor and Fields, Boston, 1854.

p. 150　Emily Dickinson. *Poems, Second Series*. Roberts Brothers, Boston, 1891. *Poems, Third Series*. Roberts Brothers, Boston, 1896.

pp. 152, 157   Nathaniel Hawthorne. Quoted by Julian Hawthorne in *Nathaniel Hawthorne and His Wife*. James R. Osgood and Co., Boston, 1885.

p. 153   Nathaniel Hawthorne. *The American Note-Books*. Houghton Mifflin Co., Boston and New York, 1900.

p. 156   Quoted by Ralph Waldo Emerson in "Visits to Concord." In *Memoirs of Margaret Fuller Ossoli*, vol. I. Phillips, Sampson and Co., Boston, 1852.

p. 159   Emily Dickinson. *Poems, Third Series*. Roberts Brothers, Boston, 1896.

p. 160   Quoted by Julian Hawthorne in *Nathaniel Hawthorne and His Wife*. James R. Osgood and Co., Boston, 1885.

p. 167   Susan B. Anthony. From a letter written to her brother, Daniel R. Anthony in 1859. Quoted by Ada Husted Harper in *Life and Works of Susan B. Anthony*, vol. I. The Hollenbeck Press, Indianapolis, 1869.

p. 170   Harriet H. Robinson. *Loom and Spindle*. Thomas Y. Crowell and Co., Boston, 1898.

p. 171   Wendell Phillips. "The Foundation of the Labor Movement," 1871. Printed in his *Speeches, Lectures, and Letters*. Lee and Shepard Publishers, Boston, 1891.

p. 174   Orestes Brownson. *The Convert, or Leaves from My Experience*. Edward Dunegan and Brother, New York, 1857.

p. 175   Theodore Parker. *The State of the Nation*. Thanksgiving Day sermon, November 28, 1850. W. Crosby and H. P. Nichols, Boston, 1851.

p. 177   William Fairfield, Quoted by Ralph D. Paine in *Ships and Sailors of Old Salem*. Outing Publishing Co., New York, 1909.

p. 178   Dr. Samuel Gridley Howe. Quoted by Harriet Beecher Stowe in *A Key to Uncle Tom's Cabin*. Sampson, Low, Son and Co., London, 1853.

p. 179   Daniel Webster. *Private Correspondence*. Little and Brown, Boston, 1857.

p. 183   William Lloyd Garrison. *The Story of His Life Told by His Children*. Houghton Mifflin Co., Boston and New York, 1894.

p. 186   Wendell Phillips. *Speeches, Lectures, and Letters*. James Redpath, Boston, 1863.

pp. 187, 188   Thomas Wentworth Higginson. *Cheerful Yesterdays*. Houghton Mifflin Co., Boston and New York, 1901.

p. 191   Thomas Wentworth Higginson. *Contemporaries*. Houghton Mifflin Co., Boston and New York, 1899.

p. 194   Henry David Thoreau. *A Yankee in Canada, with Anti-Slavery and Reform Papers*. Houghton Mifflin Co., Boston, 1881.

p. 198   Henry Adams. *The Education of Henry Adams*. Houghton Mifflin Co., Boston and New York, 1918. Copyright 1918 by Massachusetts Historical Society.

p. 199   Charles Francis Adams. *An Autobiography*. Houghton Mifflin Co., Boston and New York, 1916. Copyright 1916 by Massachusetts Historical Society.

p. 203   Thomas Wentworth Higginson. *Diary*. Quoted in *Letters of Emily Dickinson*. Edited by Mabel Loomis Todd. Harper and Brothers, New York, 1931.

p. 206   Edwin Arlington Robinson. *Children of the Night*. Richard G. Badger and Co., Boston, 1897. By permission of Charles Scribner's Sons.

p. 211   Robert Frost. *Collected Poems*. Copyright 1930, 1939 by Henry Holt and Co., New York. Copyright 1936 by Robert Frost.

p. 213   Winslow Homer. Quoted by Lloyd Goodrich in *Winslow Homer*. Macmillan Company for the Whitney Museum of American Art, New York, 1944.

p. 214   Sarah Orne Jewett. *The Country of the Pointed Firs*. Houghton Mifflin Co., Boston and New York, 1896.

p. 221   Elizabeth Reynard. Cape Cod folk tale, as told in *The Narrow Land*. Houghton Mifflin Co., Boston and New York, 1934.

p. 226   William James. Letter to his family, Christmas 1861. Quoted by Henry James in *Notes of a Son and Brother*. Charles Scribner's Sons, New York, 1914.

p. 227   Henry Adams. *The Education of Henry Adams*. Houghton Mifflin Co., Boston and New York, 1918. Copyright 1918 by Massachusetts Historical Society.

p. 231   Marsden Hartley. Quoted in *Lyonel Feininger-Marsden Hartley*. The Museum of Modern Art, New York, 1944.

p. 231   Miriam Colwell. Unpublished poem.

pp. 235, 241   Genevieve Taggard. *A Part of Vermont*. The River Press, East Jamaica, Vt., 1945.

p. 236   Amy Lowell. *What's O'Clock*. Houghton Mifflin Co., Boston and New York, 1925.

p. 240   Thomas Wolfe. *Of Time and the River*. Charles Scribner's Sons, New York, 1935.

p. 245   Justice Oliver Wendell Holmes. *Dead, yet Living*. Green, Heath and Co., Boston, 1884.

p. 246   Bartolomeo Vanzetti. *Letters of Sacco and Vanzetti*. Viking Press, New York, 1928.

p. 246   W. E. Burghardt Du Bois. *The World and Africa*. Viking Press, New York, 1947.

p. 248   Norman Corwin. *On a Note of Triumph*. Simon and Schuster, New York, 1945. Copyright 1945 by Norman Corwin.

p. 249   Conrad Aiken. "Mayflower." *Skylight One*. Oxford University Press, New York, 1949. Copyright 1945 by Conrad Aiken.

p. 250   Van Wyck Brooks. *New England: Indian Summer*. E. P. Dutton and Co., New York, 1940. Copyright 1940 by Van Wyck Brooks.